Also in this series, and by the same author and illustrator team, is *The Party Handbook*, which is filled with masses of ideas and instructions for you to create ten themed parties – from Sweetheart to Spooky, Prehistoric to Outer Space.

Join the children from *The Magic Handbook* as they and their families make simple but inspired decorations and fancy dress outfits, prepare the easy-to-make food and drinks, and play the novel party games.

What could be more fun than a fancy dress party complete with a mystifying magic show? Using both *The Magic Handbook* and *The Party Handbook* you can be certain that your parties will be ones to remember long after they are over.

THE
MAGIC
HANDBOOK

THE MAGIC HANDBOOK

BY
MALCOLM & ALAN
BIRD DART

PAVILION

WHEN YOU ARE USING SHARP SCISSORS AND
KNIVES, OR HEAT, PLEASE TAKE GREAT CARE –
AND, IF YOU THINK IT NECESSARY, ASK FOR HELP
FROM A TRUSTWORTHY ADULT WHO WON'T GIVE AWAY
THE SECRET OF YOUR TRICK.

First published in Great Britain in 1992 by
Pavilion Books Limited
196 Shaftesbury Avenue, London WC2H 8JL

A CIP catalogue record for this book
is available from the British Library.

ISBN 1 85145 597 3

Printed and bound by Kyodo in Singapore

2 4 6 8 10 9 7 5 3 1

FOR TRINA AND BARBARA, OUR MAGICAL FRIENDS,
WITH MUCH LOVE

CONTENTS

CHAPTER 1
Box of Tricks

What Every Magician Should Know

All the instructions for the magic tricks and illusions in this book have been divided into easy steps, each one accompanied by an illustration. Of course, some of the steps will need to be carried out in private before you demonstrate the trick in order for you to keep the secret of how it is done. As you gradually work your way through the steps the secret ones will soon become obvious to you. You will notice that different types of card and paper are needed, according to their thickness, for some of the tricks. All these can be bought from an art shop or a good stationers. Sometimes 'black-backed card' is mentioned, and this you will have to make yourself. Using a large brush, simply paint one side of a sheet of coloured card with black poster paint, and leave to dry before cutting out. When you are told to 'score' a line, this is to make it easier to form a crisp fold. On thin card or paper you need only draw a line with a blunt table knife along the edge of a ruler to make your score line, but on thicker mounting board you will need to use a craft knife, and maybe ask for some help from an adult.

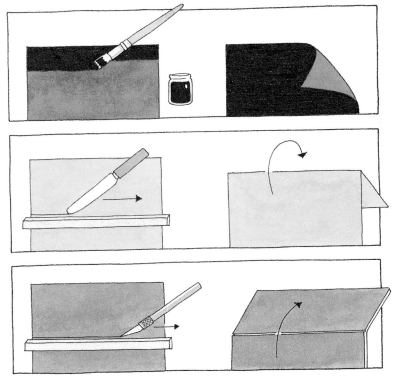

You will only need two types of glue to make up the tricks. Mostly a water-washable glue stick has been used, but where extra strength is needed a tube of clear adhesive will come in handy. Remember that any mistakes made with the clear adhesive can't be washed off, so use it very carefully and sparingly. Once you have prepared all the apparatus needed for a trick, the most important thing to do is to practise over and over again until you can perform the trick without referring to the book for help. A good way to do this is in front of a mirror — that way you will get a view of what your audience will be able to see. Remember that some of the tricks rely on you having to hide things in your hands. Very often you will be able to hold material in your palm using only your ring and little fingers, leaving your two remaining fingers and thumb free, which will look much less suspicious than a tightly clenched fist! You can get rid of any unwanted bits and pieces by quietly popping them into your pocket as you describe your next trick, or by dropping them into a box which is hidden under the table.

8

When you come to stage your magic show you will have to decide upon what to wear. On pages 76 and 77 are some suggestions for character costumes which will give your performance a really theatrical touch. You may like to theme your props so they match your chosen character by decorating them with patterned paper and paint. You will also need to think up what you are going to say as you present each illusion – this is called 'patter'. If you performed each trick without taking some time to explain or show what you were about to do, your show would soon be over, or else you would need to perform a huge amount of tricks to fill the time. Patter also makes your act more interesting, and is a useful way to 'misdirect' – which means taking your audience's attention away from what you are doing. Look through joke books and comics for funny things to say which are related to the sorts of trick you are working, talking slowly for suspense, and louder and quicker for drama. However, don't worry if you are shy – consider a mime performance, where you act in silence using exaggerated gestures, accompanied by soft music.

Sometimes you may feel that you need to enlist the help of an assistant. Choose someone you can trust, as you will have to tell them the secrets behind some of the tricks, and practise your performance together so that you both know what to do. Don't worry if a trick goes wrong – just pretend that it was part of the show, and done to check that your audience was paying attention, and go on to the next trick. On the whole, the majority of people are intrigued by magic tricks, and prepared to be baffled by them. However, sometimes you will find that there is a 'spoiler' in your audience, who will say, "I know how this one is done." You can be almost ninety-nine per cent sure that they don't know the answer (unless they have a copy of this book too), and if you challenge them they will soon make a fool of themselves with their bizarre explanation. If they persist, just wink at them and say, "Let's keep it our little secret then, shall we?" The rest of the audience will soon get fed up with them and tell them to be quiet. Above all, magic should be fun, so enjoy yourself and have a really wizard time!

The Conjuror's Workbox

To find the materials to make all the tricks in this book you need only look as far as your own home or local high street shops. You will probably have your own scissors, pens and glue already, and it's a good idea to start a workbox into which you pop bits and pieces for your trick apparatus as you collect them. Lots of materials can be found in the kitchen, writing desk and sewing basket, but make sure you ask permission first before taking them for your collection! Always buy good quality laminated playing cards — they are much easier to handle than the cheaper versions, and it won't prove to be too expensive, as you will only need three packs to play all the tricks in this book. Magicians always prefer to use real silk handkerchiefs as, when folded, they make a tiny package which can easily be hidden. Look around for other objects which can be tucked into small spaces — streamers, feathers, ribbons, confetti and chiffon scarves will all fit the bill. If you need to use a craft knife, take great care and don't store it in your workbox. Keep the blade covered when you are not using it by pushing into an old wine cork. Here is a collection of easily found items which would make a good start for your basic Magic Handbook workbox: black mounting board, black poster paint, buttons, clear adhesive, coloured card and paper, corrugated card, counters, craft knife, crêpe paper, dice, dowelling, envelopes, felt-tipped pens, gift wrapping paper, glue stick, handkerchiefs or headscarves, small and large empty matchboxes, paper clips, paper cups, plastic glasses, playing cards, rubber bands, ruler, scissors, sticky tape, table knife, tissue paper.

CHAPTER 2
Playing Cards

The Joker's Wild!

No matter how carefully the audience follow this Joker, he always manages to have the last laugh! 1. Glue a Joker and any other card to the corner of a thin envelope and leave to set. 2. Cut the card diagonally, and trim away any of the envelope showing at the corner. 3. Take three cards, two of them duplicates, and slip the Joker over one of the duplicate cards. 4. Fan the cards to show that the Joker is in the middle. 5. Close the cards and put them upside-down in your left hand. 6. Take the first card and place it face down on the table. Next take the middle card, holding back the Joker with your thumb. Now add the last card. 7. Switch all three around, then ask which card is the Joker. The choice will always be wrong.

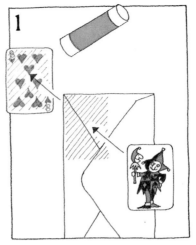

HIDE EDGE OF JOKER WITH THUMB

DROP THE JOKER OUT OF SIGHT

Thoughtwave Transfer

Thought vibrations are needed for this trick! 1. Hold a well-shuffled pack of cards, faces towards you. Sneakily glimpse and remember the bottom card. 2. Ask someone to cut the cards and place their half on the table. 3. Put your cards on top at right angles to mark the cut. 4. Say that you are now going to read your helper's mind. 5. Pick up the top pile of cards and show the bottom card saying, "This is the card you chose" – it's actually the one you glimpsed. 6. Ask him to take the card, hold it to his forehead, and concentrate very hard. You now pretend to receive thoughtwaves, and write down the number and suit on a piece of paper. 7. Show him what you have written to prove that you truly have magical powers!

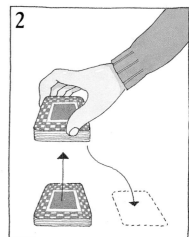

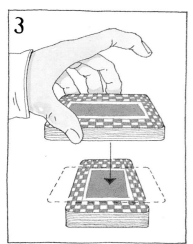

Flap Foolery

What looks like an ordinary pack of cards contains two very mystifying tricks. 1. Take two Jacks of different suits, and score and fold each one in half. 2. Glue together, then glue to the face of another card. 3. When you take the card from the pack, hold the flap down with your thumb. 4. As you sweep your arm from left to right, quickly flip up the flap and hold it down to change the card. 5. For the next trick, take two cards and fold one in half. 6. Glue half of the folded card to the back of the other. 7. Take the card from the pack, open the back flap, stand it on the table and balance any flat-bottomed article on top. 8. Swap with duplicate cards hidden at the bottom of the pack which you let the audience examine.

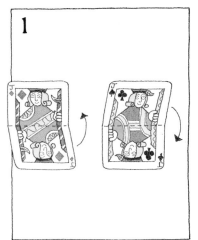

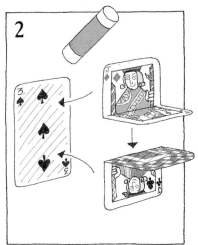

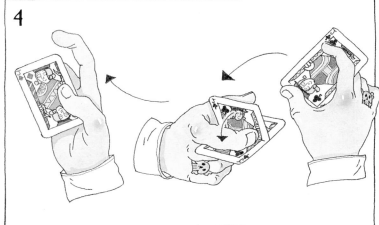

EMPTY MATCHBOX

Doubles by Numbers

Using the Science of Numerology, and a bit of magic, the card in your pocket matches one chosen by a member of the audience ... almost! 1. Take the King and Queen of Spades and draw a beard and moustache on the Queen to match the King's. 2. Return the King to the pack as the tenth card down from the top, and hide the Queen in your pocket. 3. Ask someone to give you a number between 10 and 20 (if they say 10 or 20, say, 'No, between ten and twenty'), and count out that number of cards from the pack. 4. Ask them to add the two digits together to make a single number (15 would be $1 + 5 = 6$) and count those cards off from the small pack, turning up the last card, which will be the King. 5. Now slowly pull out the disguised Queen!

1

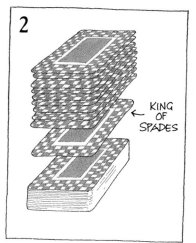

2

KING OF SPADES

3

THAT'S 13 CARDS

4

HERE'S THE FOURTH CARD

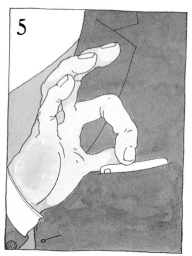

5

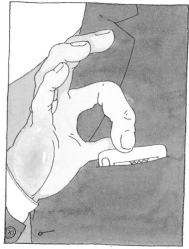

I'M SORRY, BUT THAT ISN'T THE CARD!

HMPH!

The Flying Aces

By a strange feat of magic you make two Aces disappear, and travel through thin air into your pocket! 1. You will need three pairs of Aces, and one odd Ace. 2. Keep the odd Ace separate and glue three of the duplicate Aces to the back of another, overlapping as shown. 3. Turn over and trim away excess. 4. Hide the two remaining duplicate cards in your pocket. 5. Arrange the trick card and the odd Ace in your hand and show to the audience. 6. Ask someone to examine a paper bag to make sure that it is empty, then drop the cards into it. 7. Say a magic word and take out the two cards, showing the back of the trick card to the audience. 8. Let the bag be examined again, tap your pocket and slowly draw out the missing cards.

1

2

ACE OF SPADES

3

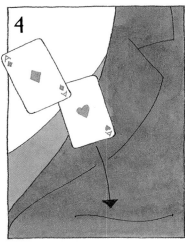

4

5

TRICK CARD

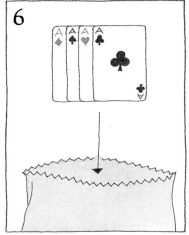

6

THIS LOOKS LIKE PAGE 91 FROM HERE

I DON'T THINK THERE **IS** A PAGE 91!

7

TRICK CARD

8

Card Detective

This is a simple trick which needs little preparation. 1. Turn the bottom card of the pack face upwards. 2. Fan out the cards, taking care not to show the end card, and ask someone to choose one (pretend you want her to take a particular card, even though it doesn't matter at all. This makes her think you've hidden a card and she'll make a point of going for another). 3. Close the pack and swap it into your other hand, turning it over as you do. 4. Ask her to remember the card. 5. Now return the card to the pack. 6. Turn your back to the audience, fan open the cards and it will be easy for you to see the chosen one, as it will be face down. 7. Turn the card round, place it sticking up out of the pack, and offer it to your helper.

WOULD YOU LIKE TO TAKE YOUR CARD, YOUNG LADY?

The Queen's Progress

Here the Queen is magically made to change places with a card held in a sealed envelope! First take two identical Queens and numerical cards from two packs of cards. 1. Cut one Queen diagonally and glue to one numerical card. 2. Glue the backs of the other two cards together. 3. Find the two cards which made a run with the numerical card, add to the diagonal card, and fan them to show the Queen in the middle. 4. Show the numbered side of the double card to the audience, seal in an envelope and ask someone to hold it. 5. Close the cards, wave them and say, "Run away, Your Majesty." Quickly turn them upside-down and fan open. 6. Now ask for the envelope, open it, and take out the double card with the Queen facing the audience.

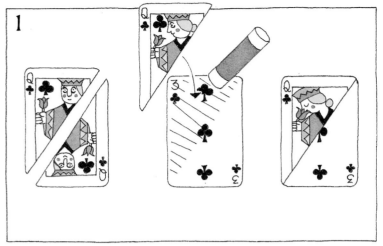

1

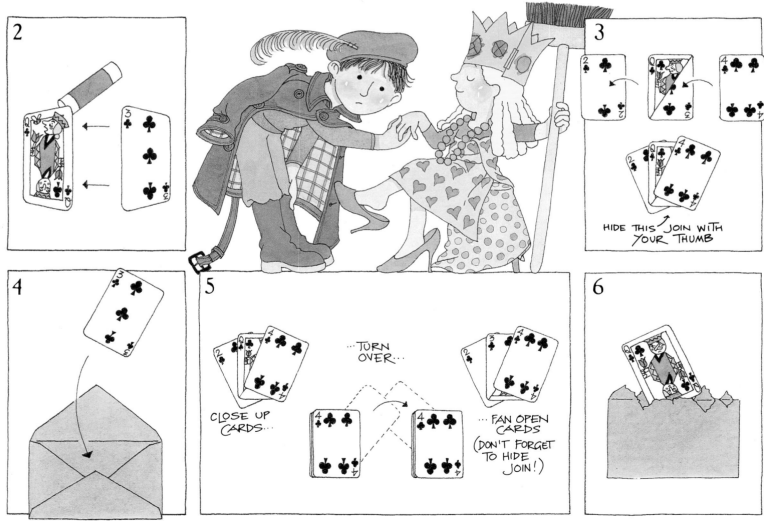

2

3

HIDE THIS JOIN WITH YOUR THUMB

4

5

CLOSE UP CARDS...

...TURN OVER...

...FAN OPEN CARDS (DON'T FORGET TO HIDE JOIN!)

6

CHAPTER 3
Magic Numbers

Dice Deduction

A very simple sum will give you the answer to this puzzle. 1. Cut two 15cm squares of card, one red and one green, and have ready some adhesive stationery dots. 2. Hand someone a red and a green dice, and ask him to throw them secretly. 3. Tell him to double the number on the red dice, add five, then multiply the result by five. 4. Now tell him to add the number on the green dice. 5. Ask him for this number, from which you must now subtract 25, leaving you with a two-figure number. 6. The first figure will be the number on the red dice, so stick that number of dots on your red card. The second figure will tell you how many dots to stick on the green card. 7. Hold up the cards to the audience — they will match the dice exactly!

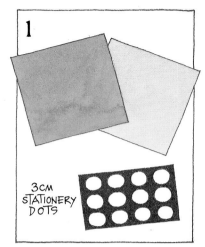

3CM
STATIONERY
DOTS

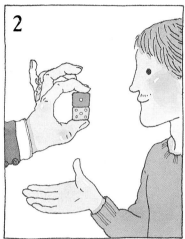

3

$3 \times 2 = 6$
$6 + 5 = 11$
$11 \times 5 = 55$

4

$55 + 4 = 59$

5

$59 - 25 = 34$

6

7

Boxing Clever

Here are a couple of crafty tricks using dice and empty matchboxes. 1. Pop two dice in a small matchbox, and take note of the numbers showing. 2. Hand the box to someone and ask her to shake it well. 3. Tell her to turn it over on to a table and slide out the tray. 4. Subtract each of the numbers you saw from seven, say them out loud, and remove the tray to prove that you are right! 5. Now glue two dice to one end of a large matchbox tray so that both sixes are upright. 6. Open the tray to show the empty end and drop in two identical dice. 7. Say that you are going to throw a double six, close the box and shake well. 8. Making sure the loose dice end up at the empty end, cast a spell and open the other end. What a wizard you are!

1 DICE MUST BE SAME DEPTH AS TRAY (SO THEY CAN'T TURN OVER!)

2

3 DICE ARE UNDER TRAY

4

5

6

7

8

The Brainy Balloon

This trick gives you the power to predict the result of a sum, using three figures chosen by your audience. 1. On a small piece of paper write '1089'. Roll up the paper, push inside a balloon and blow it up. 2. Place the balloon in full view of your audience. 3. Ask three people to give you a different single figure each, and write them down on a blackboard. 4. Reverse the numbers and subtract the smaller from the larger. 5. Now reverse this figure and add these last two figures together. 6. Pretend to write the result with your finger over the balloon. 7. Ask someone to burst the balloon with a pin and read out what is written on the paper. Only perform this trick once, as the end number is always the same.

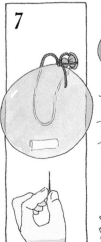

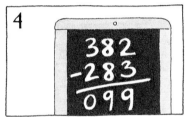

I CAN NEVER GUESS HOW THE TRICKS ARE DONE!

Some Sum!

Here you can predict the answer to a sum without knowing the numbers yet! 1. On the back page of a small note pad, which has identical front and back covers, write three three-digit numbers, trying to make the handwriting look different each time. 2. Add the figures together, write the result on a piece of paper and seal it in an envelope. 3. Hand someone the envelope to look after. 4. Open the pad at the front page and ask three people to each write a three-digit number, giving them the pen that you used. 5. Opening the pad at the back page, give it to someone else and ask them to add the numbers together. 6. Now ask the person with the envelope to open it and read out the number. Miraculously it will be exactly the same!

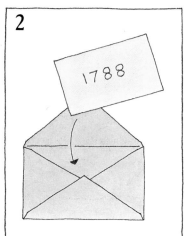

23

Count the Counters

Your audience is allowed to choose six numbers, without any persuasion on your part, and yet, once subtracted and added together, the result matches the number of counters you have selected! 1. Place a small box containing nine counters on the table. 2. Ask six people to each give you a single digit, which you write down on a large sheet of paper. 3. Now ask them to give you the same digits in a totally different order. Allow them a chance to change their minds at this point, as this will prove that they have a completely free choice. 4. Now subtract the two figures. 5. Add together all the digits of the result, then add these two digits together. 6. Finish by opening the box and counting out the counters, one by one.

1

2

398421

3

142893

4

255528

5

2+5+5+5+2+8
= 27
2+7 = (9)

6

24

Magical Multiplication

With the aid of a magic word you can make counters increase before your audience's eyes! 1. If you open a dictionary, you will find that there is a small channel behind the spine. 2. Drop five counters into this channel and close the book. The counters will now be held in place. 3. Say that you have discovered how to make extra counters, and flip through the pages until you come to the word 'multiply'. This will also prove that there is nothing hidden among the pages. 4. Next count seven counters on to the page. 5. Show a small empty basin to your audience. 6. Now pour the counters from the book into the basin, and the hidden ones will fall in too. 7. Tip out the counters and see how many more you have made.

The Lost Link and Tricky Fingers

Here you foretell the end numbers of a domino chain, and prove that you have magic fingers! 1. Remove one domino from a complete set, remember the numbers and ask someone to shuffle the rest. 2. They must fit the pieces together, matching the spots, until they make one continuous chain. 3. While they are doing this, take a 10cm × 20cm piece of black card, draw a white line down the centre and stick on stationery dots to match the missing piece. 4. When all the dominoes are down, your card will be the missing link. 5. Say that you can do all these tricks because you have an extra finger! 6. First count all your fingers. 7. Now count backwards on your right hand. Add these six to the five on your left hand and you have eleven fingers!

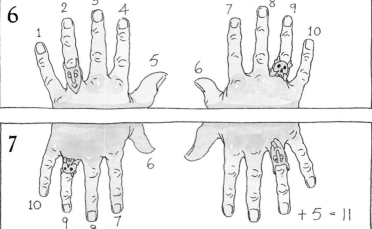

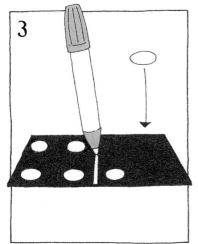

CHAPTER 4
Water Wizardry

Colourful Cocktails

You can pour three differently coloured cocktails from this magic bottle! 1. Using an enamel saucepan, simmer 200g of chopped red cabbage in 2 litres of water for 10 minutes. 2. Leave to cool, then strain into a clear bottle. 3. Dissolve 1 teaspoon of bicarbonate of soda in 100ml of warm water, and dissolve 1 tablespoon of washing soda in another 100ml of warm water. 4. Fill the hollow stems of two plastic wine glasses with the solutions, and fill a third with white vinegar. 5. Begin your performance by giving the audience three paper parasols — blue, green and pink — to examine. 6. Open the parasols and place them in the glasses as shown. 7. Fill each with the cabbage water, and watch the colour change before your very eyes.

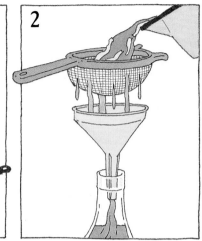

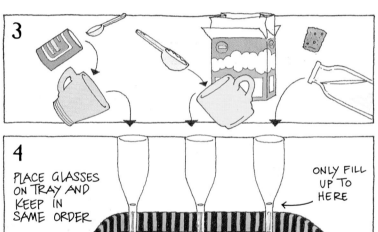

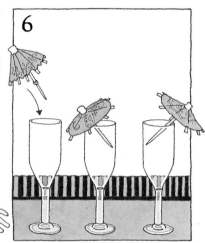

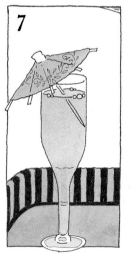

The Dissolving Coin

A coin which you 'dissolve' turns up in a peculiar place.
1. First put a handkerchief in your left pocket. 2. Ask someone for a coin, and tell them to remember its date. 3. Hold a tumbler of water in your left hand and cover it with a scarf. 4. Say you are going to drop the coin into the glass, but actually tilt the tumbler and drop the coin so it hits the outside of the glass and falls into your hand. 5. Remove the scarf and the coin will appear to be in the glass. 6. Cover again and place on the table, keeping the coin in your left hand. 7. Say a magic word, remove the scarf, and the coin has gone! 8. Take the handkerchief from your pocket and pretend to sneeze. 9. Open the handkerchief, drop the coin, and check the date.

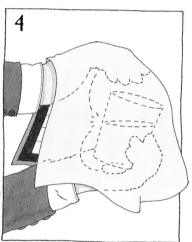

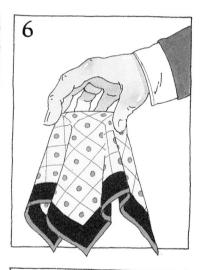

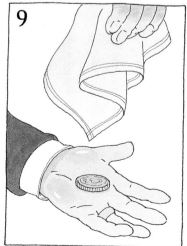

LOOK - IT IS MY 1992 COIN!

Gravity-Defying Water

With your magic skills you can make water stay in a glass — even when it's upside-down! 1. Buy a sheet of acetate from a model shop and cut two circles — one a bit larger than the top of a glass, and the other to fit inside the top. Glue the circles together and leave under a book to set. 2. Cut a square of paper, 5cm larger than the lid, wet it and place the lid in the middle. 3. Let someone examine the glass, then fill it with water. 4. Place the paper on the glass, making sure the lid fits exactly over the top. 5. Hold the paper down and turn the glass over quickly. 6. Peel off the paper and the water will stay in place. 7. Holding over a bowl, slide your hand down the side of the glass, and the lid and water will fall out.

2

DAMPEN PAPER UNDER WATER

4 LID HIDDEN UNDER PAPER

THREE THINGS, BECKY! — MORE PRACTICE, TEST IT FIRST OVER THE BOWL, AND SAY SORRY TO SAFFRON!

Water on the Elbow

This is a handy way to recycle water in a shortage!
1. Carefully make a 5mm hole in the side of a plastic funnel with a pair of scissors. 2. Cut two circles of thin plastic — one to fit the base of the funnel, and the other to fit just above the hole. Make a hole in the smaller circle with a thick needle. 3 Fix both pieces in place with waterproof bath sealant and leave to set. 4. Fill the funnel with water through the side hole and plug with a bit of modelling clay. 5. Ask for a thirsty helper and give him some water to drink. 6. Say that you've run out of water for the next trick, hold the funnel to his left elbow and pump his right arm up and down. 7. Pick off the clay and the water will trickle out into a waiting bowl.

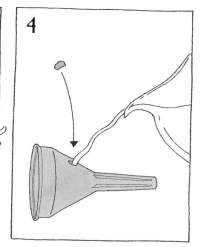

BE **VERY** CAREFUL WHEN USING POINTED SCISSORS

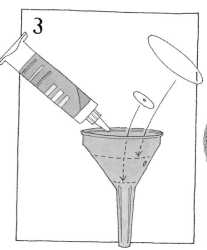

WOULD YOU GO ON TO THE NEXT SQUARE, PLEASE — WE'RE HAVING A PARTY IN THIS ONE!

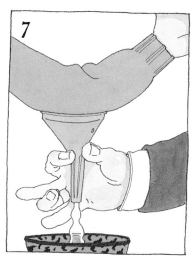

The Water Pipe

With the help of a magic tube you can make a cup of water empty and refill in a flash. 1. Take two paper cups and trim away the top of one so that it fits inside the other without being seen. 2. Make a tube to fit loosely over the cup from a rectangle of thin card. 3. With the lining in place, half fill the cup with water. 4. Hold in the left hand and cover with the tube. 5. Say a magic word and lift off the tube, fingers inside and thumb outside, gripping the lining with your fingers against the side of the tube. 6. Place the tube and lining on the table and show the empty cup. 7. To make the water reappear, pick up the tube and lining together and fit over the cup. 8. Whip off the tube and the water is back where it began!

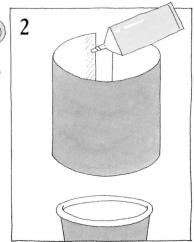

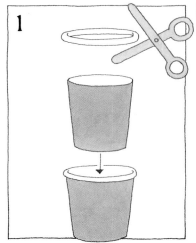

Liquid Paper

A flick of a scarf, and confetti is changed into water.
1. Cut a circle of thin card to cover the top of a paper cup. Also cut two circles of corrugated card to fit inside the top. 2. Glue the circles together, then paste confetti over the top. 3. Half fill the cup with water, fit the lid on top, and place in a card box. 4. Fill the box with confetti. 5. Take an identical paper cup, scoop up some confetti, and let it fall back into the box. 6. Fill the cup again, but this time swap it with the hidden one. Brush off any loose pieces of confetti and place the cup on the table. 7. Cover with a scarf. 8. Cast a spell, take off the scarf together with the top, and throw them into the box. 9. Now slowly pour the water into a bowl.

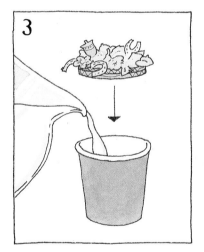

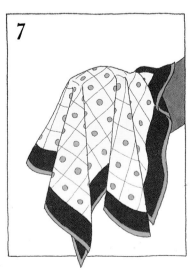

33

The Soggy News

This is a very thirsty newspaper! 1. Glue the pages of a newspaper together along the spine. 2. Open the paper towards the back. Fix the top of a self-seal food bag in line with the top edge of one page with double-sided tape. 3. Now stick another piece of tape on the opposite side of the bag, draw a line of glue down the side and across the bottom of the page, and close the paper. 4. Open the bag and pop in a thin washing-up sponge. 5. Show the paper and open it at the centre pages. 6. Roll the paper into a cone. 7. Stir your hand inside the cone to open the bag top. 8. Slowly pour in about 100ml of water. 9. Unroll the paper and refold it, closing the bag top at the same time. 10. Now open the paper – the water has gone!

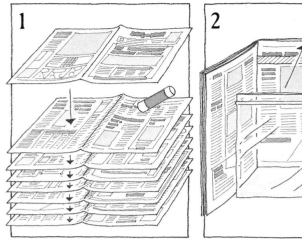

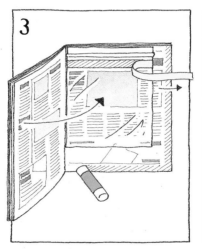

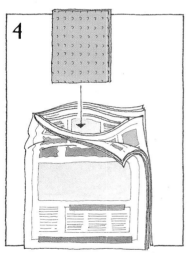

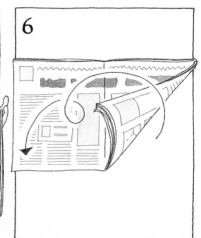

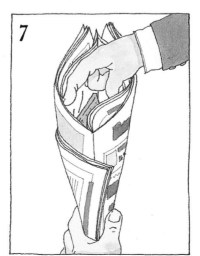

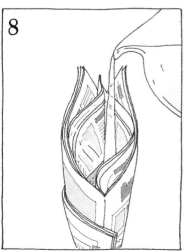

RUN FINGER ALONG TOP
TO CLOSE BAG

CHAPTER 5
Bewitching Bafflers

The Foxing Box

Any small object placed inside this mysterious box can be made to disappear and reappear to order. 1. Remove the tray from an empty box of household matches, cut away one end and paint the inside black. 2. Glue 5mm wide strips of board to the inside top edge on all three sides. 3. Taking measurements from inside tray, cut another tray from black card and score folds. 4. Glue together and glue card tab to back. 5. Slide into outer tray and glue on bead handle. 6. Cover box sleeve with coloured paper and insert tray. 7. Open drawer, drop in object then close. 8. Say magic word and open drawer, holding tab on inner tray. The drawer is now empty! Close drawer and open again without holding tab to make object reappear.

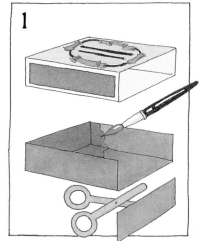

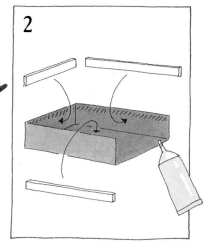

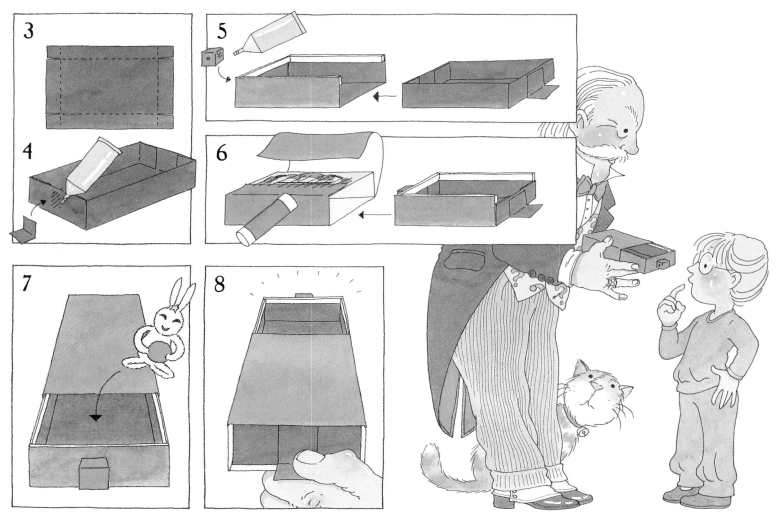

The Curious Changing Bag

With this versatile little bag you can make things appear and disappear, change colour, or alter completely. 1. Cut three 25cm squares of felt, sew together on three sides and trim with braid and tassels. 2. You now have a bag with two compartments. 3. Sew a button on to a square of fabric, secretly drop it into one compartment, and hold top edges together. 4. Turn other compartment inside out to prove that bag is empty. 5. Drop a button, thread and fabric into empty compartment and cast spell. 6. Reach in bag and pull out sewn-on button. 7. Turn bag inside out to show that it is still empty, holding top edges of full compartment together. You can now make string knot itself, scarves change colour, and toy rabbits disappear!

1

HAND OVERSEW, OR MACHINE STITCH, CLOSE TO EDGE

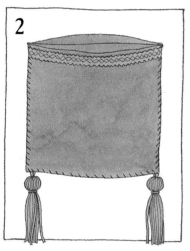

2

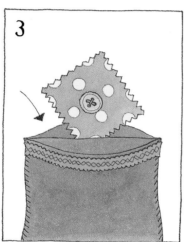

3

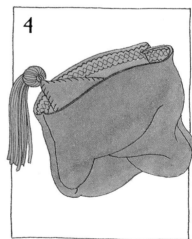

4

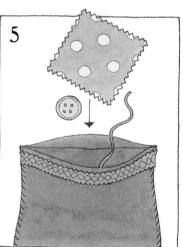

5

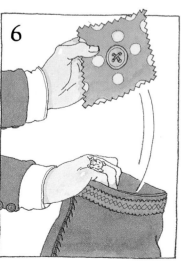

6

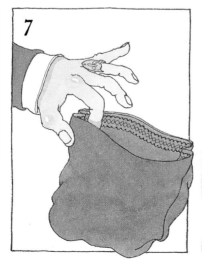

7

MUM SAYS CAN YOU DARN THESE SOCKS, NOW, PLEASE?

Thin-Air Tubes

From these two empty tubes you can produce an endless number of surprises. 1. Glue two pieces of black-backed card into tubes, overlapping by 1cm. 2. Make another tube from black card and cut 1cm tabs round base. 3. Fold tabs and glue to card base, then tape opened-out paper clip to top. 4. Slip tubes over each other, and hang drum inside. 5. Glue ends of six streamers together to make one long streamer, and drop inside drum. 6. Keeping the hook towards you, slide the inner tube downwards and show that it is empty. 7. Slide it back up inside the outer tube. 8. Now slide the outer tube downwards and show that it is empty. 9. Slide it back up. 10. Hold both tubes together and slowly draw out the streamer from the hidden drum.

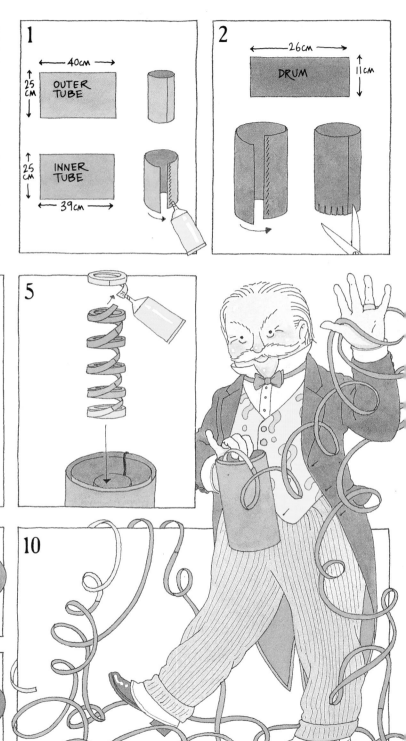

The Bunny Hoop

A tube and a hoop of paper are all that's needed to produce ribbons, and an extra guest! 1. Glue a rectangle of black-backed card into a tube, overlapping by 1cm. 2. Cut rabbit from felt and draw features with felt-tipped pens. 3. Fold 2m lengths of ribbon zigzag fashion, and fold the rabbit in half twice. 4. Sandwich ribbons and rabbit between a 15cm circle and a 25cm square of wrapping paper, and glue edge of circle. 5. Fit package inside a 12.5cm embroidery hoop, where it will look like a single sheet of paper. 6. Show the empty tube to the audience, and let them see both sides of the hoop. 7. Fit hoop on top of tube. 8. Say a magic word and break the paper. 9. Draw out the ribbons, followed by your new pet!

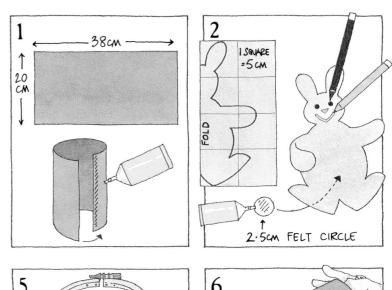

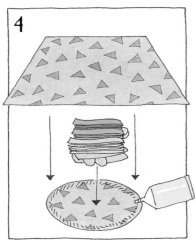

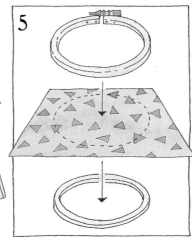

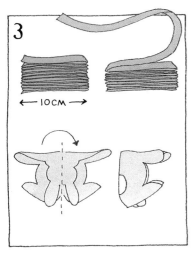

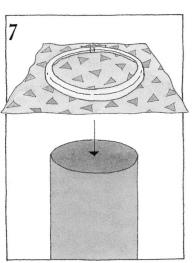

A Handy Palette

You can mix lots of different colours once you know this secret. 1. Find a thimble to fit your index finger, with a little room to spare, and paint it flesh-coloured. 2. Cut strips of tissue paper in blue, yellow and green. 3. Pleat the green strip, leaving 7cm at one end unfolded. 4. Fold the end as shown and place the thimble on top. 5. Trap the ends inside the top with your finger. 6. Now drape a scarf over your other hand and make a well in it with your index finger, leaving the thimble as you do. 7. Push the two short strips into the hidden thimble, and say that you can mix them. 8. Insert your finger and draw out the thimble. 9. Ask what blue and yellow make, pull out the magically mixed strip, and show the empty scarf.

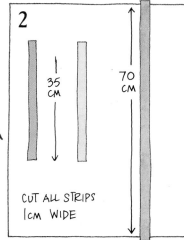

1

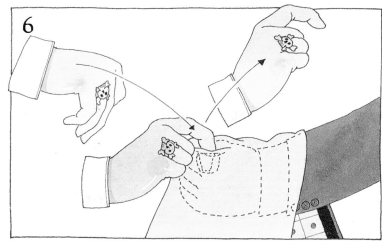

2

35 CM

70 CM

CUT ALL STRIPS
1CM WIDE

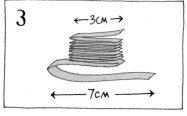

3

←3CM→

←7CM→

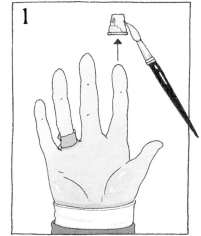

5

THEN BEND
FINGER
INTO PALM
TO HIDE
THIMBLE

6

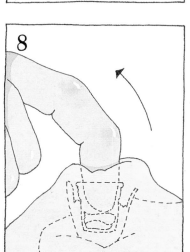

7

PUSH TISSUE
DOWN WITH
LITTLE
FINGER

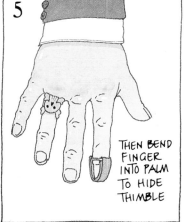

8

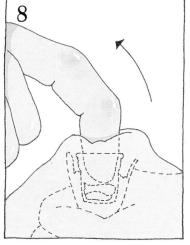

9

The Invisible Mender

Once you have mended this rope you will never find the join! 1. Sew the ends of a 15cm length of cord together to make a loop. 2. Take a piece of elastic the length of your arm and sew the loop to one end. 3. Thread the elastic up your sleeve so the loop is just inside your cuff, and fix with a safety pin. 4. Pull out the trick loop and place it in your hand. 5. Fold a 1m length of matching cord in half and hold the looped end. 6. With your other hand pretend to draw up the loop, but really pull up the trick loop. 7. Now ask someone to cut through the loop. 8. Cover your hand with a scarf, cast a spell, and release the loop, which will vanish up your arm. 9. Remove the scarf, and let the 'restored' rope be examined.

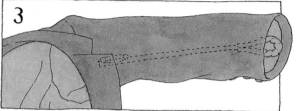

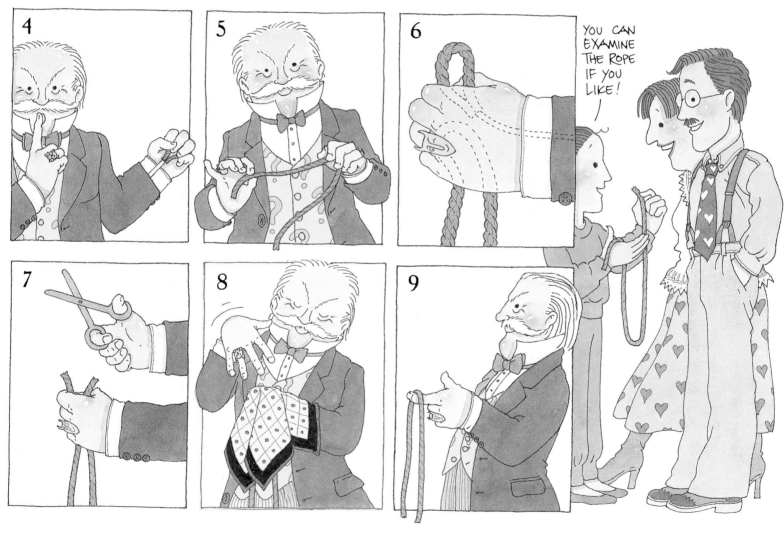

YOU CAN EXAMINE THE ROPE IF YOU LIKE!

The Sorcerer's Ark

This box will vanish or change whatever you drop inside!
1. Cut all the pieces from black mounting board, then score the back of the large rectangle. 2. Fold box sides and join ends with sticky tape. 3. Glue card strips 3cm up from one end. 4. Glue base piece on top of strips. 5. Attach lid with sticky tape. 6. Paint cut edges and back of flap with black poster paint. 7. Cover box with gift wrap and add a tassel to the lid. 8. Slot tab at base of flap through slit in box base. 9. Now open the box to show that it is empty, and pop in some coloured feathers. 10. Close the lid and secretly move the tab at base of box. 11. Open the lid and the feathers will have disappeared! How about trying to make them change colour next time?

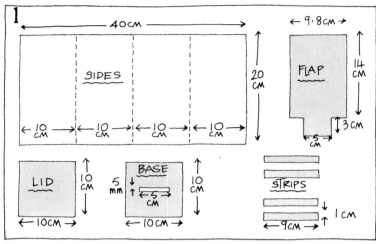

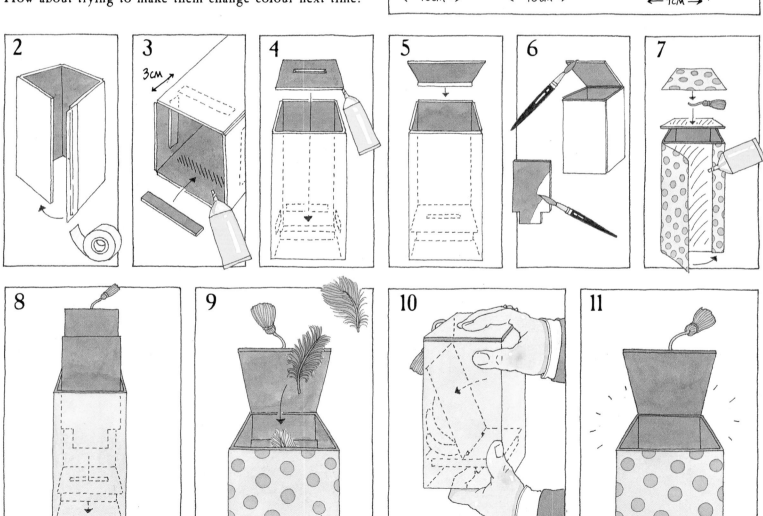

CHAPTER 6
Mystic Mindreading

Fingertip Readers

Even though there is no way an ordinary person can see through an envelope, your X-ray eyes allow you to read five sealed cards and match them to the people who wrote them! 1. Before your performance take five envelopes and make a tiny snip on each flap with a pair of scissors. Each snip will be in a different position so that you will be able to tell one from another. 2. Ask five people to draw up their chairs in a line. 3. Keeping the envelopes in order, hand them out, giving the one with the right hand snip to the person on the far right of the line, and so on. 4. Now hand a blank card and a pencil to each person and ask them to sign their name on the card and then seal it securely in their own envelope. 5. Ask someone to collect all the envelopes and to shuffle them vigorously to make sure that they are well and truly mixed up before handing them back to you. 6. It will now be a simple task for you to identify the owner of each envelope, as the marks will correspond to their position in the line of chairs, but to make it look difficult you must do a bit of acting. Staring at the back of the envelope, pretend to draw out the name with your fingertips, and place them to your forehead in thought. You can now call out the person's name and tear open the envelope to prove that you are correct. To make your act seem more convincing you could occasionally pretend that you are only getting part of the name, or an initial, before finally receiving the correct information.

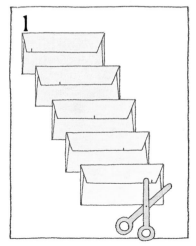

I CAN SEE AN 'S' OR AN 'H'

THE NAME IS 'HARRY'!

Harry

Sensory Detection

In spite of being blindfolded for this experiment, you are still able, using a combination of colour vibrations and extra-sensitive fingertips, to detect which envelope holds the odd-coloured button. 1. You will first need to prepare a trick envelope. Remove one envelope from a set of five identical ones, carefully spread glue diagonally across the inside of one corner and leave until set. 2. Place all five envelopes on your table, with the trick envelope at the bottom of the pile, together with four red buttons, one green button and a scarf. 3. Hand the top four envelopes to four members of the audience and ask each one to drop a red button into their envelope and then seal it. 4. Now let them examine the green button, pointing out that it is exactly the same size, shape and weight as the red ones, open the trick envelope and allow them to drop the button inside and seal the flap. 5. Shuffle the envelopes well so that it is now impossible to know which one contains the green button, keeping all the top edges together. 6. Ask someone to blindfold you with the scarf and to hand you the envelopes. By holding each envelope by the top edge in turn, and shaking it briskly from side to side, you will soon be able to detect the odd one out, as the green button won't be able to roll into the glued corner. 7. When you have found the trick envelope announce that this is the one containing the green button, whisk off your blindfold, tear open the envelope, and hold up the button to prove your genius.

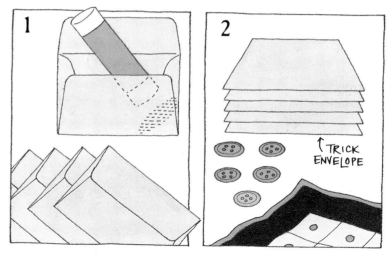

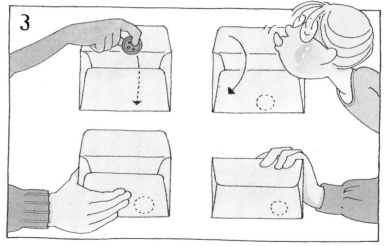

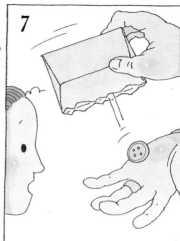

Menagerie Mystery

In this trick your psychic powers appear to guide you so that you are able to correctly predict the name of an animal which will be chosen completely at random by a member of your audience. 1. Have a small pad and a pencil ready and ask your audience to call out names of animals. As each name is called you appear to write it down on the pad — but what you really do is write down on each sheet the first animal name which was called out! 2. If you want to fool your audience a little, ask them to spell any particularly unusual names, or to describe what their animal looks and sounds like. 3. As you write about a dozen names, tear off the sheets of paper and fold each one in quarters. Drop them all into a little basket and shake them about to make sure that they are very well mixed. 4. Now announce that you are going to make a prediction. Pretend to concentrate very deeply, then secretly write the same animal name on another sheet of paper, seal it in an envelope, and give it to someone to hold. 5. Take one of the pieces of paper from the basket, unfold it, and pretend to read out one of the animal names someone called out (but not the one written down) just to prove that everything is above board. 6. Offer the basket to a spectator and ask them to choose one of the papers, then tell them to unfold it and read out what is written. 7. Now ask the person holding the envelope to open it and read what is written on the piece of paper inside. Miraculously, the two names are exactly the same!

Colour Control

You will always be able to predict which of three very different colours your volunteer has chosen if you follow this illusion carefully. 1. To start off with you will need to cut three 10cm squares of card – one purple, one green and one orange. On the back of the purple card write 'You will choose purple', and on the back of the green and orange cards write 'You will not choose this colour'. 2. Find an envelope that the three cards will fit inside, and find a smaller envelope that will fit inside also. Into this small envelope seal a slip of paper on which you have written, 'You will choose orange'. 3. On the front of the small envelope write 'You will choose green', then slip the envelope and the cards into the large envelope. 4. Start by removing the three cards from the envelope. Hold them up to the audience (making sure that they can't see the writing on the backs) and ask someone to choose a colour. 5. If purple is chosen, you simply turn over all three cards and let the messages be read. The trick is now complete. 6. However, if green is chosen, don't turn over the cards, but pick up the large envelope and remove the smaller one, showing the message written on the front, and say, "You chose green because you are under my influence!" 7. But if orange is chosen, leave the cards as before, take out the small envelope, without letting the audience see the message, open it and read what's on the slip of paper. Now you can say, "I was able to enter your mind, and that's why you chose orange!"

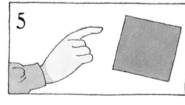

Cards in Mind

You will need to enlist the help of an assistant for this trick, and let them into the secret – but make them swear never to tell anybody, otherwise you'll turn them into a toad! 1. Take a pen with a removable cap and scratch five marks with a sharp nail on the pen barrel, just below the cap. 2. Now take the four Aces and one Joker from a pack of playing cards, and find an envelope to fit them. 3. On the front of the envelope write, 'Diamonds, Spades, Hearts, Clubs, Joker', and place the pen inside your pocket, together with a small piece of paper. 4. Tell your audience that, after many hours of meditation, you have developed the power to transfer thoughtwaves between yourself and a chosen assistant. Now ask your partner to leave the room. 5. Tell your audience to choose one of the playing cards and seal it in the envelope, and ask them to make sure that it can't be seen through the envelope. 6. Now write down the name of the card on your piece of paper, craftily replacing the pen's cap with the clasp opposite the mark that corresponds with the card's position on the list – e.g. Clubs is the fourth word, so the clasp should be opposite the fourth mark. 7. Call in your partner and give her the envelope and pen. Hold the paper to your forehead and ask her to concentrate on your thoughts. 8. After a bit of play-acting she removes the pen's cap, taking note of the clasp's position, and underlines that word on the envelope. You can now open the envelope to prove that two minds are better than one!

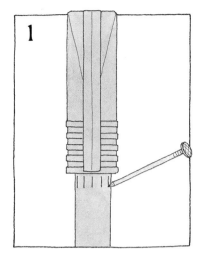

Message Revelation

This is another trick in which you will need to find an assistant trustworthy enough to share the secret with you. Before the show starts, you must both decide upon, and remember, a message which he will write later. 1. To begin the demonstration, hand out a piece of paper, a pencil and an envelope to each member of your audience, including your assistant. 2. Tell everyone to write down either their name, a question, some numbers, or a phrase on the paper, and then to seal it in their envelope. 3. You now collect all the envelopes, taking your helper's last and placing it at the bottom of the pile. 4. As you return, with your back to the audience, hide the last envelope in a pocket, or under your skirt or trouser waistband. 5. Now is your chance to play the part of a great actor! Hold the top envelope to your forehead and pretend to read it with your mind. 6. Once you are sure that you have 'received' the message correctly, call out the message you and your conspirator have decided upon, he agrees that he wrote it, and you open the envelope to confirm — but what you really see is the next person's message, which you now memorize. Take the next envelope from the top of the pile and continue with your 'reading' display until all the envelopes have been opened. 7. One person will now be bound to say that their message hasn't been read so, after a short search, discover the missing envelope and 'read' the message as before. End by passing the basket round, allowing the messages to be examined.

1 SECRET ASSISTANT

2

3 ASSISTANT'S ENVELOPE

4

5

6 THIS ONE SAYS 'HOCUS POCUS'

WOW! I WROTE THAT!

2+2=4

(DROP MESSAGES FACE DOWN IN BASKET ONCE READ)

7 HEY! YOU MISSED OUT MINE!

NOW, HOW DID IT GET <u>THERE</u>?

'GENTLEMEN PREFER BLONDES'

VERY TRUE!

HOCUS POCUS

Treasure Trove

From a collection of a dozen matchboxes you are able, through your supernatural powers of persuasion, to influence a member of your audience into choosing the only box holding hidden treasure. 1. Ask someone for a ring and place it in one of twelve empty matchboxes. 2. Taking note of this box, and placing it in the position shown, spread them all out on a table in two rows, six boxes in each row. By asking the following simple questions, you always interpret the answer to refer to the block of boxes not containing the one with the ring. For example, if the front row is chosen, you can take it to mean the front row as seen by you, or the front row as seen by them. The same also applies to back, left and right! 3. First ask whether the front or back row should be removed, and take away the complete row of empty boxes, leaving six on the table. 4. Now separate the boxes into two sets of three and ask whether the right or left set should be removed. Again take away the three empty boxes. 5. You now have three boxes left (the one with the ring should be in the middle) from which you ask for one to be chosen. If the middle one is selected, give it to your helper to hold and remove the other two. 6. Should one of the side boxes be chosen, remove it and ask for a choice between right or left so that you can take away the remaining empty box, leaving the one containing the ring. 7. Whatever the outcome at this last stage, the resulting box will surprisingly always hold the treasure!

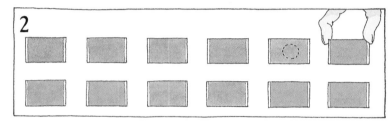

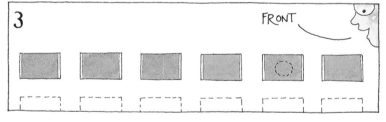

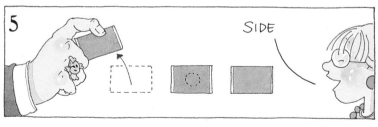

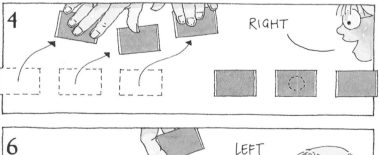

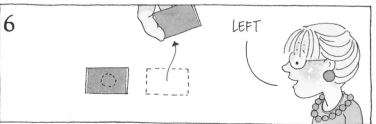

CHAPTER 7
Hanky Panky

The Elusive Button

An ordinary button, folded inside an equally ordinary handkerchief, disappears without trace and defies logic.
1. Stick a small piece of double-sided sticky tape across one corner of a patterned handkerchief. 2. Have a button ready and let it be examined. 3. Hold up the handkerchief (covering the tape with your hand) and show the front and back to your audience. 4. Lay it on the table with the taped corner nearest you, and place the button in the middle. 5. Fold over the taped corner and press on to the button. 6. Repeat with the other three corners. 7. Cast a spell and pick up the last corner to unfold the hankie. 8. Now pick up the corner with the button, together with another, and display your perfectly empty handkerchief!

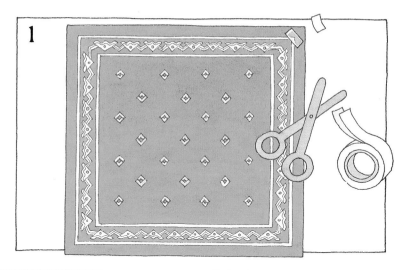

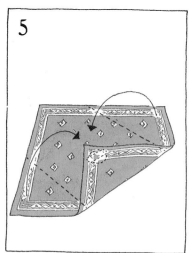

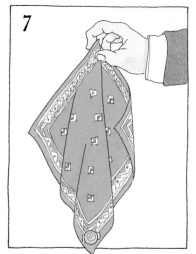

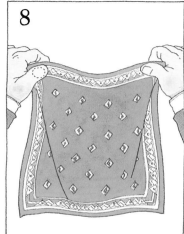

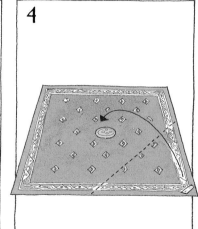

LOOK, DANIEL— IT'S JUST A REGULAR BUTTON!

Hideaway Handkerchief

A tiny doll disappears into this handkerchief, and will only reappear when you say a magic word! 1. Find a small beige rubber band and secretly slip it over your index and middle fingers. 2. Drape a 50cm hankie over your hand, slip your thumb into the rubber band and stretch it open wide. 3. Push the doll inside the well made by the rubber band until it disappears. 4. Draw out your fingers and thumb so the band snaps shut above the doll, trapping it in place. 5. Quickly toss the handkerchief between your hands several times, proving that the doll has vanished. 6. Now scrunch the hankie in your hands, cast your spell and gently pull the fabric open. The doll will pop out of the well, and the rubber band will fly away unnoticed.

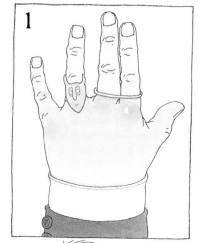

Break Time

Everything is not as it appears when you use this magic scarf. 1. Take a 50cm square of printed cotton and hem two opposite sides by turning under 5mm, then 2.5cm, and sewing down. 2. Repeat with the other two sides. 3. Feed a wooden cocktail stick down one of the open hems until it reaches the middle. 4. Now place the scarf flat on the table, with the hem containing the stick nearest you, and drop another cocktail stick in the centre. 5. Fold the scarf in three . . . then three again. 6. Hold the scarf by the top edge and give it a quick shake so the loose stick drops to the base. 7. Ask someone to snap the stick in the scarf (giving him the hidden one to break). 8. Open out the scarf, and the stick has been magically restored!

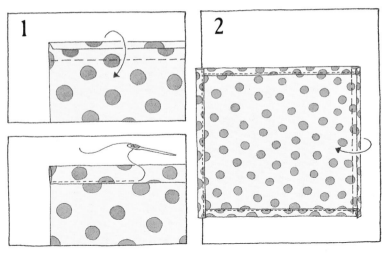

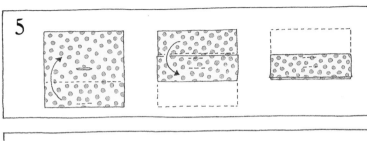

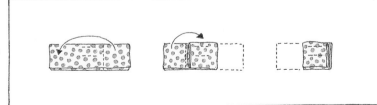

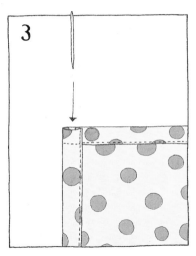

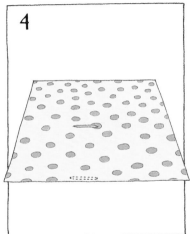

Switching Shades

A quick flick, and this handkerchief will change colour before your eyes! 1. Take two 50cm squares of silk in different colours, and neatly hem the raw edges. 2. Place together, stitch across one corner as shown, then trim close to the sewing line. 3. Turn to the right side and thread through a 2cm curtain ring. 4. Handsew the ring in place. 5. Catch the squares together in the centre with a few stitches. 6. Now fold diagonally and oversew all four side edges together. 7. Next take corner A of the inner square and thread it up through the ring so that it just shows. 8. Hold the ring in your hand and display the handkerchief. 9. Now pull up the corner with your other hand – the hankie will turn inside out and change colour.

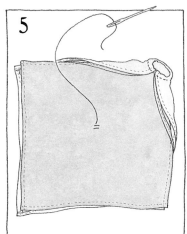

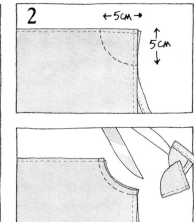

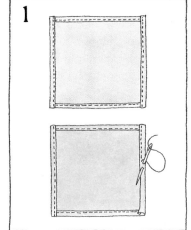

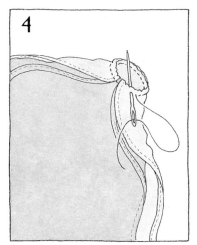

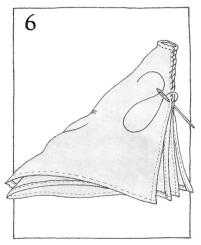

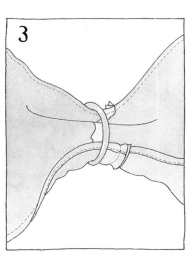

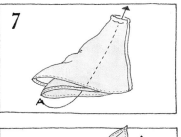

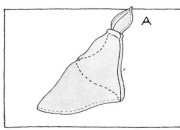

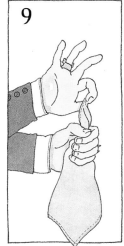

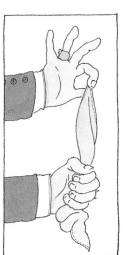

The Sneaky Scarf

This very useful hankie is the secret behind a host of disappearing and transforming tricks. You will need two identical patterned cotton handkerchiefs and some iron-on hemming tape. 1. Arrange strips of the tape on the back of one handkerchief as shown. 2. Now gently lay the other hankie on top so that you don't disturb the tape, then carefully iron to melt the tape's glue. 3. You will find that there is now a secret pocket in one quarter of the handkerchief. 4. To make something disappear, fold into four (with the pocket on top) and hold by the corners. 5. Drop the top corner and place the object in the pocket. 6. Hold both corners of the pocket with your other hand, shake out the hankie, and the object will have vanished!

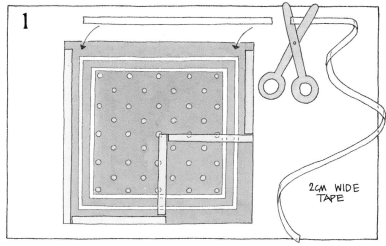

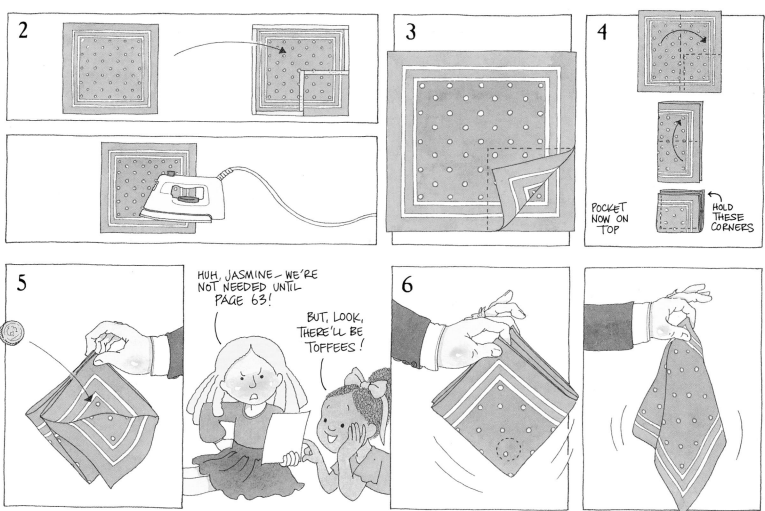

56

Tumbler in Transit

Can you guess how to make a tumbler disappear simply by covering it with a handkerchief? You will need another two patterned hankies, iron-on hemming tape and some cardboard. 1. Cut a circle of card exactly the same size as the top of a plastic tumbler. 2. Place the circle on the back of one handkerchief and arrange strips of the tape as shown. 3. Top with the other hankie and iron to bond together. 4. Sit at your table and place the tumbler in front of you. 5. Now cover it with your handkerchief, making sure that the card sits on the rim. 6. Holding the top, slide the tumbler backwards so that it slips off the table and into your lap. 7. Hold the hankie up high, give it a quick shake, and, hey presto, the tumbler has gone!

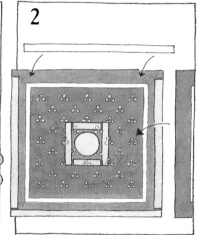

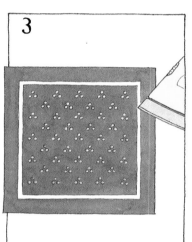

The Wizard's Wallet

With this tricky folder you can change the colour of silk scarves, or even turn plain into patterned! 1. Take two large card envelopes and cut off the flaps. 2. Place them on top of each other with the openings at opposite ends and join the sides with sticky tape. 3. Cover the outside with wrapping paper. 4. You've now made a tube with a hole down the middle and a secret compartment at each end. Tuck a spotty scarf into one compartment. 5. Squeeze the sides to open the wallet, show it to your audience and draw a plain scarf through the middle. 6. Open the tube again, making sure the empty section is at the top, and push the scarf and some felt spots into it. 7. Now you can draw out the 'newly spotted' scarf from the base!

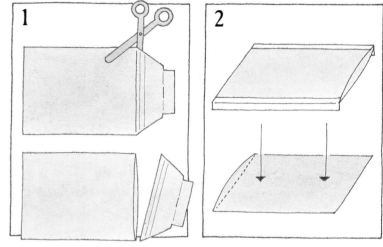

CHAPTER 8
Wonderful Wands

Mysterious Moves

A wand sealed in one envelope mystically reappears in another! 1. Make a basic wand by cutting a 30cm length of 1cm diameter dowelling. Paint 4cm at each end white, and the rest black. 2. Wrap a 30cm x 4cm piece of black paper round the wand and glue to make a tube which will slip off easily. 3. Glue a 4cm square of white paper around each end. 4. Now rattle the wand about inside a large empty envelope. 5. As you draw it out, let the wand slip from inside the tube and into the envelope. 6. Seal the flap. 7. Next show another empty envelope, drop the wand tube into it and seal. 8. Cast a spell and screw up the second envelope, proving that the wand has gone. 9. Then open the first envelope and remove the travelling wand.

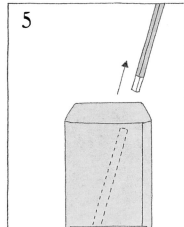
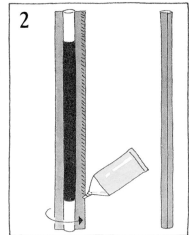
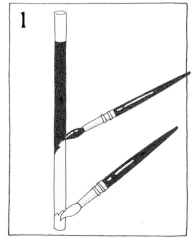

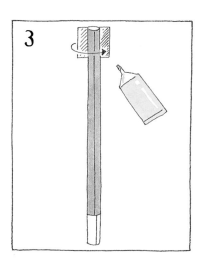

Hoodoo Hues

Magicians can NEVER decide what colour their wand should be! 1. Using the basic wand, make a tube as before with a 26cm × 4cm piece of red paper, and glue a 4cm square of white paper round one end. 2. Form another tube over the red one, using a 26cm × 5cm piece of blue paper, and glue a 4cm × 5cm piece of white paper round one end. 3. Slide the tubes on to the wand as shown. 4. Hold the end of the red tube, say that you'd like a colour change, and wrap the wand in a piece of red tissue paper. 5. Draw out the wand, leaving the blue tube inside, and screw up the paper. 6. Saying that black is smarter, after all, hold the end of the wooden wand and wrap it in black tissue. 7. Draw out the wand, leaving the red tube behind.

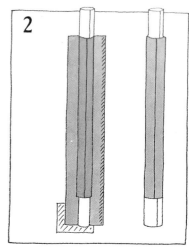

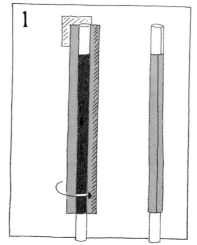

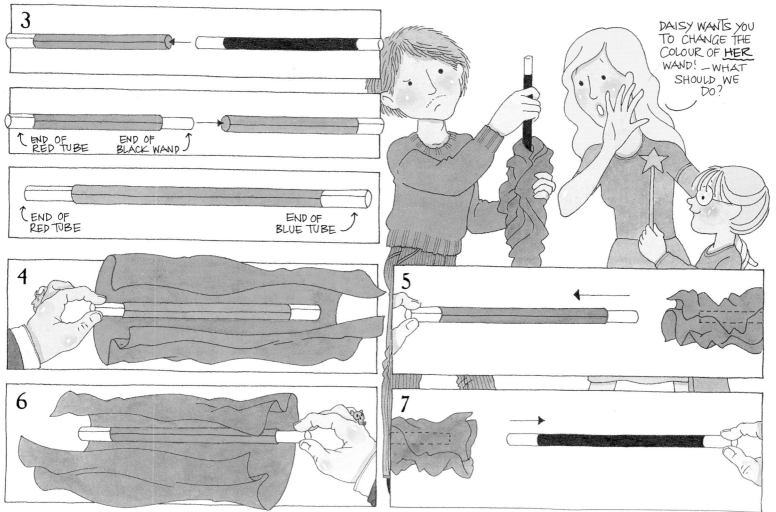

END OF RED TUBE

END OF BLACK WAND

END OF RED TUBE

END OF BLUE TUBE

DAISY WANTS YOU TO CHANGE THE COLOUR OF **HER** WAND! —WHAT SHOULD WE DO?

61

The Elastic Enigma

This solid wand will stretch and shrink before your very eyes! 1. Cut a 30cm length of 1cm diameter dowelling and paint it black. 2. Wrap and glue a 4cm square of white card round one end. 3. Wrap another 4cm square of card round the wand, and glue edges together to make a tube which will slide up and down freely. 4. At each end glue an 11mm circle of card. 5. Slide the tube up to the fixed end, hold it in your hand, and feed the rest of the wand up your sleeve. 6. Now you can slowly draw out the wand, holding on to the tube until it reaches the other end. 7. To make the wand disappear into a ball of yarn, hold the tube and push the fixed end into the ball. 8. Slide the tube down the wand, feeding the wand up your sleeve.

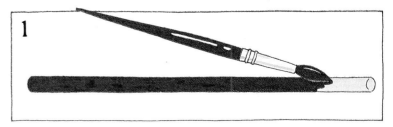

1

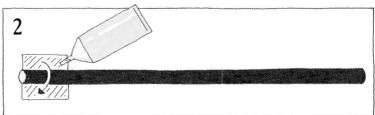

2

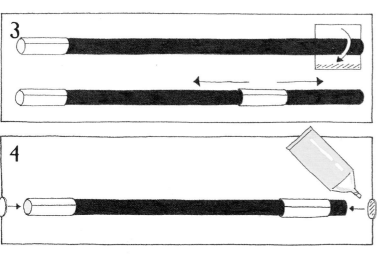

3

4

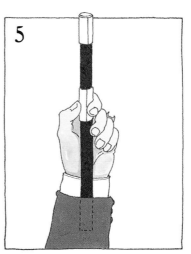

5

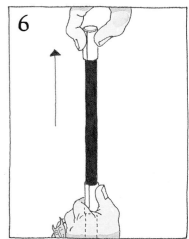

6

7

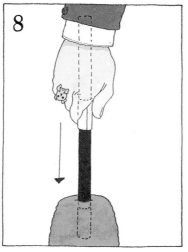

8

PLEASE MAY WE HAVE OUR WAND BACK, GRAN?

A Sweetie Sorter

Here's a way to pick out your favourite toffees. 1. Paint a 30cm length of 12mm dowelling black, and screw a 12mm ring magnet to one end. 2. Glue a 4cm square of white card round each end. 3. Now glue a 13mm circle of card to each end. 4. Unwrap a red toffee and tape another magnet to the wrapper. 5. Re-wrap the toffee and place it in a bowl with some differently coloured ones. 6. Now offer the wand to someone so they take the magnetic end in their hand, and ask them to pick out the red toffee for you with the tip of the wand. 7. Of course, they won't be able to. 8. Take the end of the wand from them, and it will be easy to pick out your toffee with the magnetic tip. 9. Unwrap the sweet, screw up the paper, and enjoy!

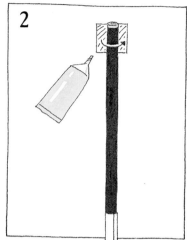

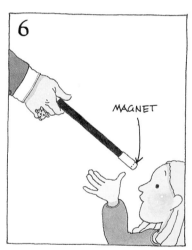

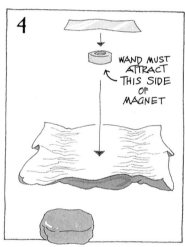

WAND MUST ATTRACT THIS SIDE OF MAGNET

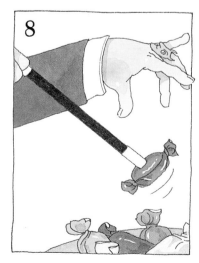

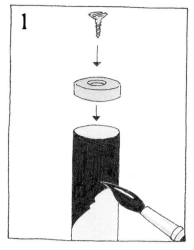
MAGNET

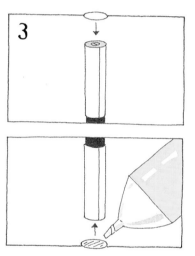

MY YOUNG ASSISTANTS WILL NOW MAKE THE OTHER TOFFEES DISAPPEAR ONE BY ONE

Spellbinding Levitation

Make sure you keep your distance from the audience for this trick, for your reputation hangs by a thread! 1. Make another 30cm wand from 1cm dowelling, paint it black and glue 4cm paper squares round each end, then push a 1cm white drawing pin into each end. 2. Cut a 1 metre length of transparent sewing thread and knot the ends round the drawing pins. 3. Now lay the wand on the table and, without people noticing what you are doing, slip the thread round the middle finger on each hand. 4. Ask for complete silence, fix the wand with a piercing stare, and draw your hands slowly apart. 5. The wand will start to rise, and float between your hands. 6. To end, flick the thread off your fingers and catch the wand as it falls.

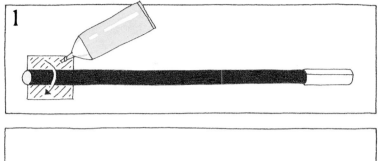

Hypnotic Hand and The Rising Wand

Your wand can also be trained to cling to your hand in a trance, and come when you call! 1. Using the drawing pin wand, tie one end of a 70cm length of transparent sewing thread to a drawing pin, and tie the other end round your trouser button. 2. Now push in a map pin, halfway along the wand. 3. Put the wand into your pocket, making sure the pin is hidden. 4. Start by bringing out the wand, trapping the pin between your index and middle fingers. 5. Slowly raise your hand so that the wand is vertical – it doesn't drop off! 6. Tug the pin out of the wand and pop it somewhere safe. 7. Now drop the wand into an empty wine bottle, putting in the tied end first. 8. Move the bottle away from you and the wand will rise to your order.

2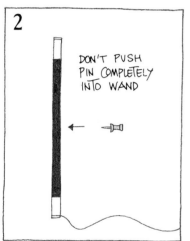

DON'T PUSH PIN COMPLETELY INTO WAND

3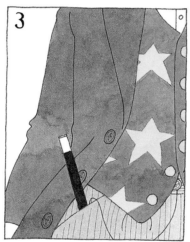

4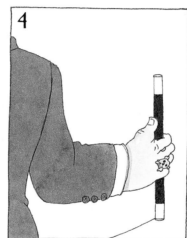

5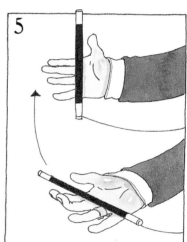

6

7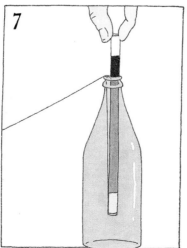

8

The Jumping Rod

At your command this wand will jump out of your hand.
1. Drawing-pin a 20cm length of elastic to one end of a 15cm piece of 1cm diameter dowelling. 2. Wrap and glue a 30cm x 4cm piece of black paper round the dowelling to make a tube, placing the dowelling at one end of the paper. 3. Glue a 4cm square of white card round each end of tube, then glue an 11mm circle of card to the solid end. 4. Find a 12mm metal button with a shank and paint it white with model enamel. 5. Mark a point on the elastic 5mm in from the wand's end. 6. Sew this point to the button and trim off excess elastic. 7. Trap the button between your index and middle fingers, stretch the elastic and hold the wand. 8. As you let go of the wand it will jump!

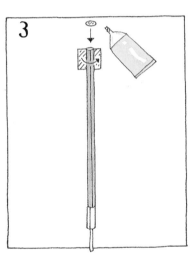

3MM WIDE ELASTIC

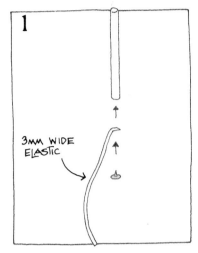

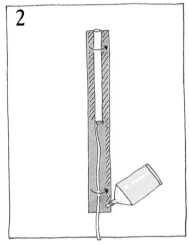

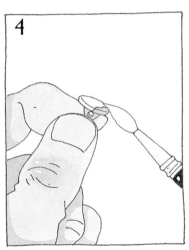

5 MM

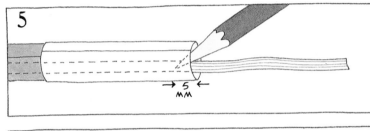

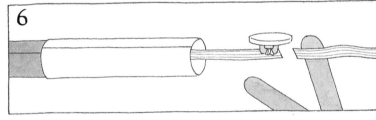

CATCH IT, SAM!

CHAPTER 9
Paper Puzzlers

The Loopy Loops

Four paper bands, which you say are identical, give very surprising results when they are cut in half! 1. Cut 5cm wide strips from folded crêpe paper, then cut each strip into 1 metre lengths. 2. Glue the ends of one strip together. 3. When this band is cut down the centre you get two equal thin bands. 4. Twist the strip once before gluing. 5. Cut down the middle and you get one long thin band. 6. However, if you cut one third in from the edge you are left with one long and one short band ... joined together! 7. Twist the strip twice before gluing. 8. This time you get two equal bands joined together when you cut down the centre. Ask for a volunteer to help cut the bands and wait to hear their cries of utter amazement!

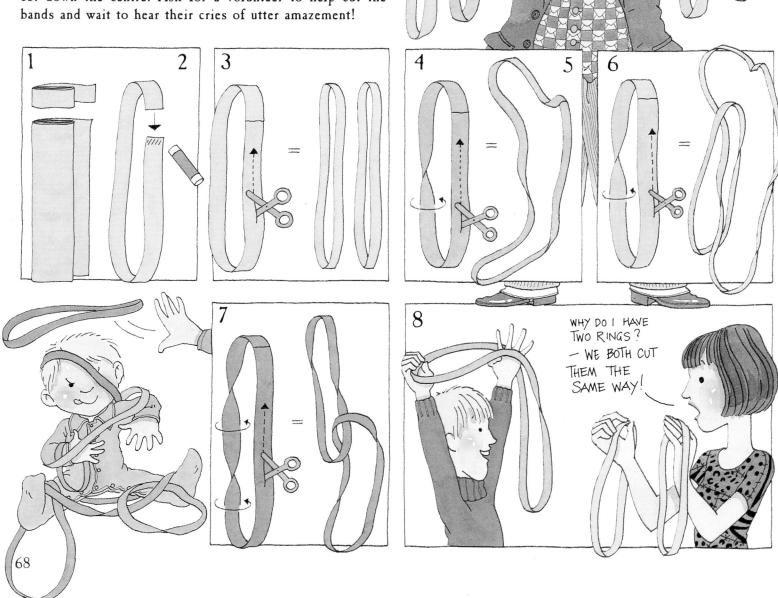

WHY DO I HAVE TWO RINGS? — WE BOTH CUT THEM THE SAME WAY!

The Peculiar Paper Package

With what looks like an ordinary sheet of paper you can make coins, or small flat objects, disappear into thin air. 1. Cut two 20cm squares of paper and stick together in the centre with a dab of glue. 2. Fold in the sides on one sheet. 3. Now fold in the top and bottom. 4. Turn the sheet over so the folded piece is hidden. 5. Ask someone for a coin, place it in the centre of the top sheet and wrap it up by folding the sheet as before. 6. Pick up the package, wave it around, say a magic word, and turn it over before placing it back on the table. 7. When you open the paper the coin has disappeared! Make the coin reappear in the same way. Why not make buttons change colour by first popping one into the secret package?

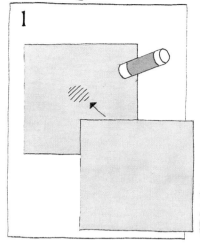

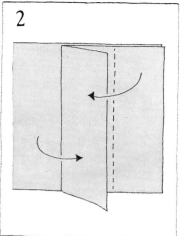

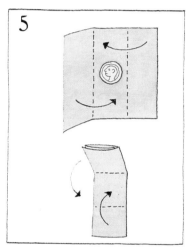

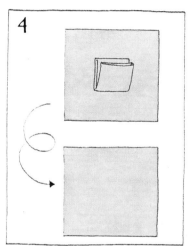

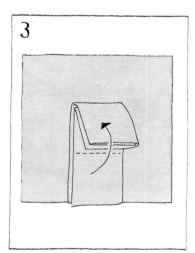

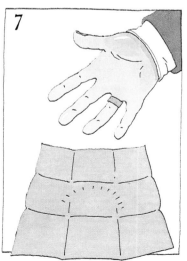

WHAT HAVE YOU DONE WITH MY LUCKY RED BUTTON?

Check This!

Here's an easy way to make patterned paper from plain.
1. Cut three 20cm squares of tissue paper, one black and two red. On one red square draw 2.5cm checks with a felt-tipped pen, and leave until dry. 2. Glue the checked and black squares together with a spot of glue at one corner. 3. Accordian pleat the checked square along the vertical lines. 4. Now pleat this piece to make a tiny package. 5. Holding the package at the back, show the black and red squares. Place them together, tear in half vertically, place together and tear in half again. 6. Now repeat by tearing these strips in half and half again. Push all the pieces into one hand. 7. Blow on them, then slowly pull out the corner of the checked square and open it fully.

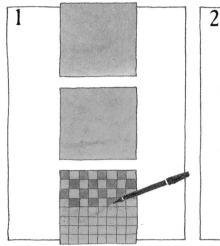

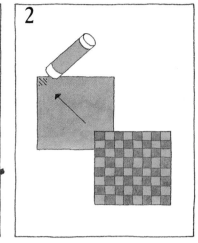

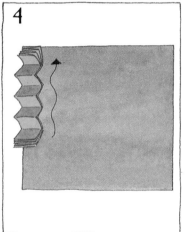

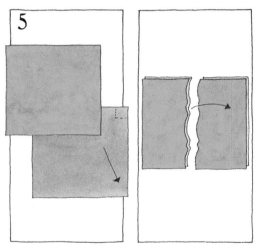

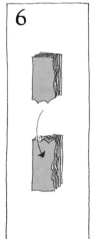

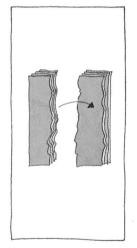

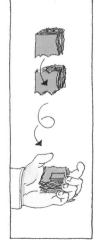

I DON'T THINK BLOWING WILL HELP, NOW YOU'VE TORN THEM UP!

THAT'S BRILLIANT!

70

Chain Reaction

Paper chains are so simple to make using this method!
1. With eight 15cm x 2.5cm strips of wrapping paper, make a paper chain in two colours. 2. Flatten each link to form a cross-shaped package. 3. Tape a small rubber band to one end. 4. Now tape a small coin to the other end, then cover with a piece of matching paper. 5. Fold over the side tabs of the cross to make a neat packet. 6. Slip the rubber band over your middle finger and hide the package in your palm. 7. Show two 30cm x 2.5cm strips of paper in both colours and tear into quarters. 8. Roll up and tuck into your palm behind the folded chain. 9. Wave a glue stick 'wand' and, keeping your hand cupped, throw the package sharply. The coin will make the chain open out.

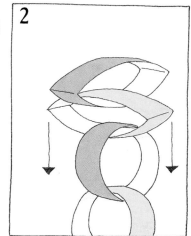

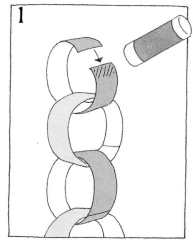

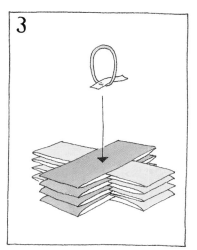

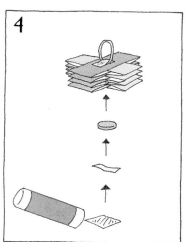

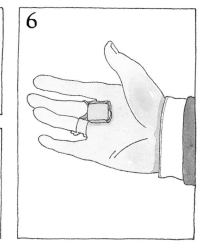

The Illogical Hole

With a few crafty snips you are able to push back the boundaries of reasonable thinking. 1. Show your audience a playing card, and say that you are able to cut a hole in it large enough for you to climb through. 2. First fold the card in half lengthways and make seventeen cuts, 5mm apart, starting at the folded edge and ending each one 5mm short of the outside edge. 3. Now turn the card round and make more cuts in between, starting from the outside edge and finishing 5mm short of the folded edge. 4. Carefully unfold the card and make one cut along the fold line, keeping both end strips intact. 5. Gently open out the card, taking care not to tear it, and you'll have a hoop big enough to pass right over your head and body!

72

Burst and Bewilder

This magic bag really goes with a bang! 1. You will need two identical paper bags. Cut small snips along the base of one bag, and trim off 2cm from the top edge. 2. Cut tiny diamonds, spades, hearts and clubs from paper and drop into the other bag. 3. Now place the trimmed bag inside the other one, glue the top edges of the two bags together, and trim level with pinking shears. 4. Begin by showing your audience the inside of the bag to prove that it is empty. 5. Drop in four playing cards, one from each suit, then blow up the bag and cast a magic spell. 6. Burst the bag between your hands and the pips will 'drop' off the cards and float gently to the ground. Now screw up the bag, and don't let anyone inspect the evidence!

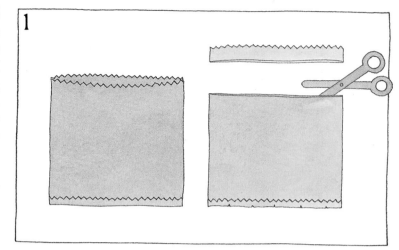

1

2

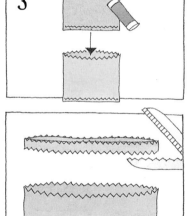

3

4

AN EMPTY BAG— HOW INTRIGUING!

5

6

Cunning Clips and Tumbler's Bridge

These two tricks prove the magic power of paper. 1. Slip two large paper clips on to a 20cm × 5cm piece of paper exactly as shown, and ask if anyone knows how to link the two clips without removing them from the paper. 2. First slide the right-hand side of the strip under the left clip. 3. Turn the paper over and repeat by slipping the right-hand side under the left clip. 4. Now, if you take the two ends of the strip and pull sharply the clips will fly, linked together, into the air! 5. For the second trick ask someone to make a bridge between two tumblers with a 20cm × 10cm piece of writing paper, strong enough to support another tumbler. 6. When they have given up, accordian pleat the paper, and it will hold the tumbler.

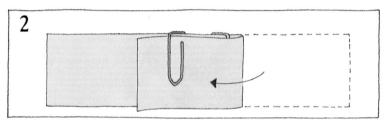
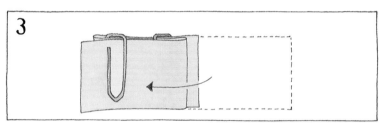

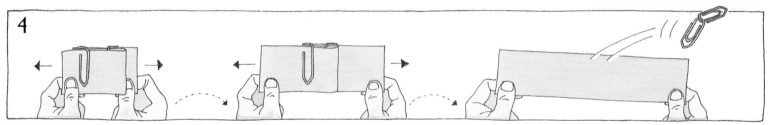

CHAPTER 10
For Your Amazement!

Looking the Part

Conjuror

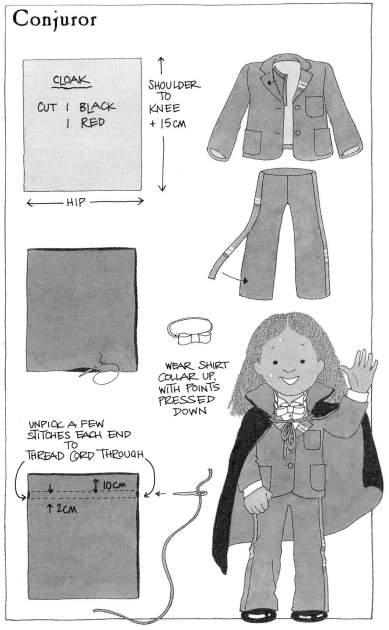

CLOAK

CUT 1 BLACK
1 RED

SHOULDER TO KNEE + 15CM

← HIP →

WEAR SHIRT COLLAR UP, WITH POINTS PRESSED DOWN

UNPICK A FEW STITCHES EACH END TO THREAD CORD THROUGH

↕ 10CM
↑ 2CM

Cut satin slightly larger than jacket revers, fold under raw edges and sew in place. Sew satin ribbon down sides of trousers. Make a loop of elastic to fit round neck and sew on a ribbon bow. Sew cloak pieces together, leaving a space open, turn to right side and join opening. Work two rows of stitching, unpick ends and thread casing with cord.

Enchanter

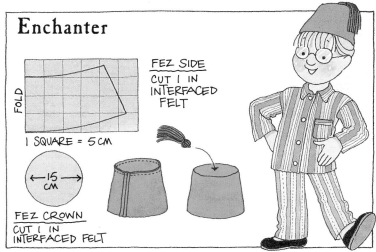

FOLD

1 SQUARE = 5CM

FEZ SIDE
CUT 1 IN INTERFACED FELT

← 15 CM →

FEZ CROWN
CUT 1 IN INTERFACED FELT

Taking 6mm turnings, join sides of fez and press seam open. Now, with right sides together, sew crown piece to top edge, then turn through to right side. Sew a silky tassel to top of hat. Wear with striped pyjama jacket and trousers, in different colours, and button the jacket right up to the neck. Finish off with black canvas pumps.

Mystic

TURBAN
SEMICIRCLE
← HEAD + 3CM →

GATHER THIS EDGE

ADD BEADS AND BROOCH

Neaten base of turban with a small hem, then fold in half with right sides together. Gather curved edge, taking large stitches, draw up tightly and secure. Turn to right side and decorate with a brooch and some feathers. Unpick the collar from an oversized shirt, then trim away tails and cuffs and hem raw edges. Tie a silk sash round waist.

Oriental

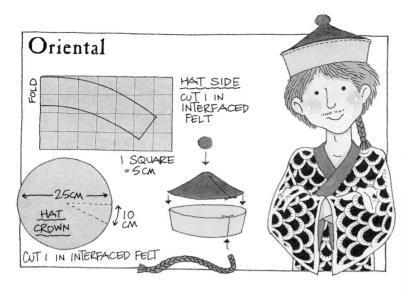

FOLD

HAT SIDE
CUT 1 IN
INTERFACED
FELT

1 SQUARE = 5 CM

25 CM

HAT CROWN

10 CM

CUT 1 IN INTERFACED FELT

Taking 6mm turnings, join sides of hat and dart in crown, then press seams open. With wrong sides together, sew crown to top edge of hat, then top with a woolly bobble. Make a 20cm long plait, using 24 strands of black double knitting yarn, secure end and sew to back of hat. Wear with a patterned dressing gown or kimono, and trousers.

Mime Artiste

DAISY
FOLD 10CM
PAPER SQUARE
INTO QUARTERS

FOLD
DIAGONALLY
AND
CUT
PETALS

4 CM

Wear a stripy long-sleeved tee shirt, together with thick black tights, held up by clip-on braces. Slick back hair with gel. Colour face white, and draw on a surprised expression, using face paints. Have ready a large jacket in case you intend to perform any tricks which need wide sleeves or pockets, and pin a paper daisy to the lapel.

Wizard

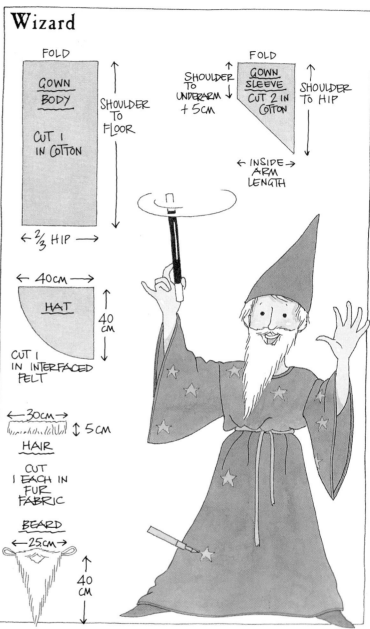

FOLD

GOWN BODY

CUT 1 IN COTTON

SHOULDER TO FLOOR

⅔ HIP

FOLD

SHOULDER TO UNDERARM + 5CM

GOWN SLEEVE
CUT 2 IN COTTON

SHOULDER TO HIP

INSIDE ARM LENGTH

40CM

HAT

40 CM

CUT 1 IN INTERFACED FELT

30CM

5CM

HAIR

CUT 1 EACH IN FUR FABRIC

BEARD

25CM

40 CM

Sew sleeve heads to gown body, then join side and sleeve seams and hem raw edges. Cut neck opening to fit over head and bind with bias tape. Draw stars with gold marker pen, and tie a cord round waist. Join hat sides to form a cone, adjusting to fit head, and turn to right side. Glue fur fabric hair to hat, and sew elastic ear loops to beard.

77

The Black Hole Table

Every magician needs a table upon which to demonstrate their tricks. Although you can use any ordinary table, this one is a trick in itself, as it contains a secret bag, and the long skirt provides a space where you can store and hide props until they are needed. 1. First cut two 60cm squares of corrugated cardboard from large packing cases and glue them together with paper paste, arranging the squares so that the ridges in each piece are at right angles to one another. Leave under heavy weights until completely dry. 2. Now, with a craft knife, carefully cut a 20cm square hole in the centre. 3. Tape two or three grocery cartons together to reach a good workable height, then glue the tabletop to the flaps of the open top carton. 4. Cut an 83cm x 30cm piece of black velvet for the secret bag. With right sides together, and taking a 1.5cm seam turning, join the short sides. 5. Now make four 1cm-deep cuts, 20cm apart, along the top edge of the bag, then gather the base edge tightly and secure. 6. Glue the top edge of the bag to the opening in the tabletop. 7. Glue a length of satin or taffeta lining, wide enough to reach the floor, round the table, placing the selvedge at floor level and cutting away excess. Trim the hem with fringing. 8. Now cut a 58cm square of black velvet. Cut out a 22cm square hole in the centre, glue to the tabletop, and leave until set. 9. Taking 5 metres of 2cm-wide flat braid or ribbon, glue to the tabletop in a grid pattern, covering all the raw edges of the fabric.

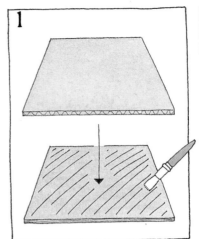

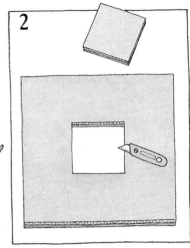

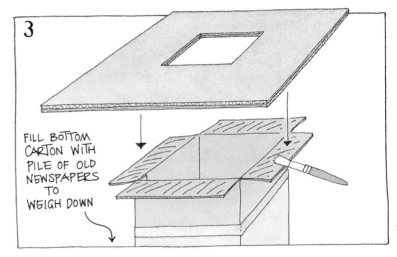

FILL BOTTOM CARTON WITH PILE OF OLD NEWSPAPERS TO WEIGH DOWN

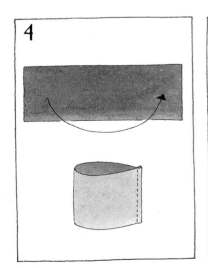

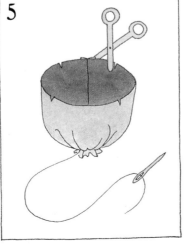

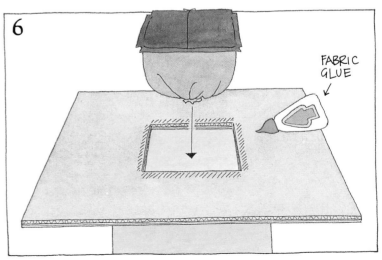

FABRIC GLUE

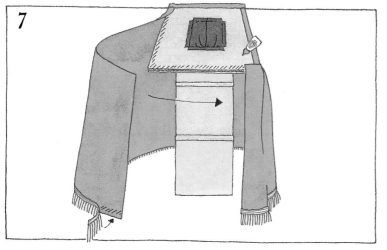

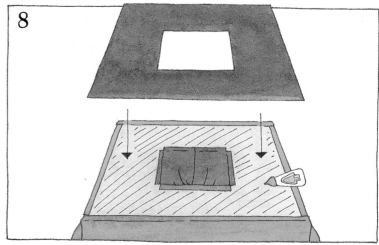

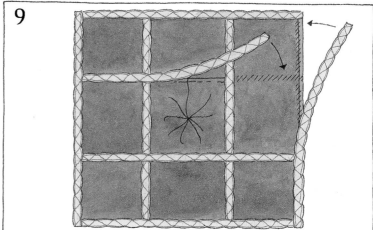

Black velvet is one of the magician's favourite fabrics as it absorbs the light, and this table will appear to your audience to have a completely flat top. You alone will know that the centre square contains a bag, in which you can either hide objects you want to produce later, or secretly drop unwanted pieces of equipment once you have demonstrated a trick. The tumbler on page 57 could be dropped into the bag instead of your lap, as could the map pin in the Hypnotic Hand trick on page 65. To make something appear, you need only drape a hankie over your hand, position it above the bag, and slowly draw out whatever you have hidden beforehand. Now turn the page to find a top hat which will increase your magic repertoire.

The Tip-Top Hat

From this hat you will be able to produce enough objects to fill it to overflowing! 1. Cut the brim, crown and flap pieces from black mounting board, and the side piece from black cover paper. 2. Cut a 10cm square hole in the centre of the crown. 3. Now paint all the white sides and edges with black poster paint. 4. Attach the flap to the crown with sticky tape to form a hinge. 5. Score 1cm in from top and bottom edges of side piece, then cut small tabs down to score lines and fold back. 6. Roll and glue the side piece into a tube, overlapping by 1.5cm. 7. Glue the bottom tabs to the crown, and the top tabs to the brim. 8. Open out a paper clip and tape to the back of the flap. 9. When the hat is placed on a flat surface the flap will open by itself. Hide lots of paper lanterns (weighted with coins to make them open automatically), streamers, and scarves in your magic table's bag. Show that the hat is empty and position it over the edge of the bag to open the flap. Now draw out all the hidden bits and pieces, until your table is completely covered, then pile everything back into the hat and take a bow!

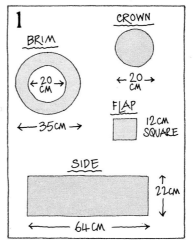

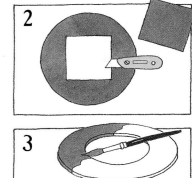

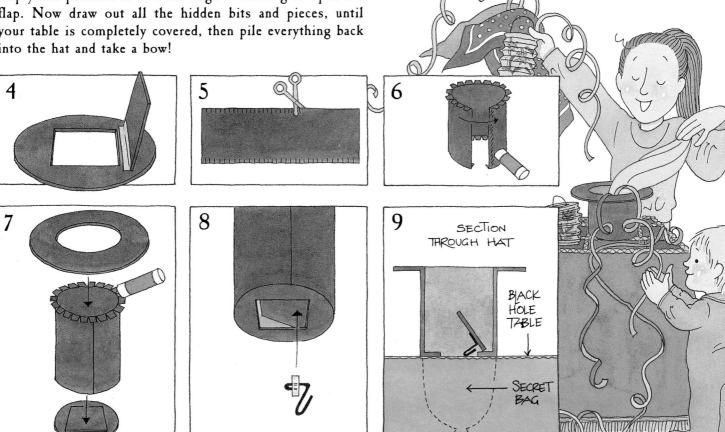

CHAPTER 11
Party Magic

Party and Show Invitations

Juicy Ink

Squeeze a lemon, or cut a potato in half and scrape the cut surfaces to produce juice, and put this invisible ink into a saucer. Write your party invitation on paper with a wooden cocktail stick dipped in the juice, and leave to dry. Include a message telling your guest to develop the note by warming it in a 275°F/140°C oven until legible.

Moving Image

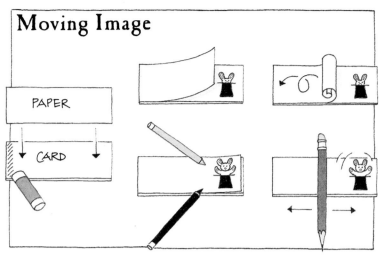

Cut two 15cm × 5cm rectangles – one in card, one in paper – and glue together along one short side. Draw a bunny peeping out of a hat on the card piece. Trace the hat through on to the paper, then draw the bunny further out of the hat. Roll the paper tightly, and give instructions to slide a pencil across the top to make the bunny move.

Pop Up

Cut a 30cm × 20cm piece of coloured paper and fold it into quarters to make a card. Open, then score and fold the diagonal lines as shown. Draw a dove on a piece of folded white paper, cut out and colour, and glue behind the inside top edge. Re-fold, write your party details inside the card, and stick stationery stars on the front.

Candle Writing

Sharpen the end of a white candle into a point, using a blunt knife, and trim away the wick. Now use your candle 'pencil' to write the invitation on a piece of paper. Add a note in ordinary pencil to let your guests know that the writing will be revealed if they scribble over it with a felt-tipped pen (which you may also like to enclose).

Tabletop Trickery

Card Markers

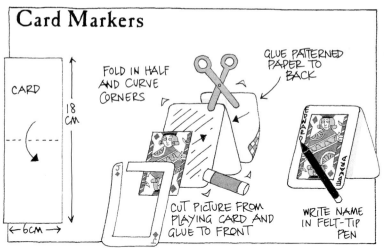

CARD

18 CM

6 CM

FOLD IN HALF AND CURVE CORNERS

GLUE PATTERNED PAPER TO BACK

CUT PICTURE FROM PLAYING CARD AND GLUE TO FRONT

WRITE NAME IN FELT-TIP PEN

Top Hat Bowl

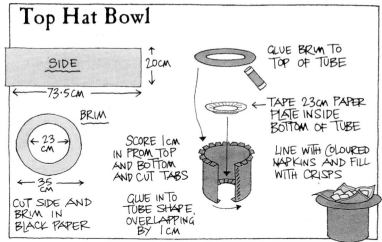

SIDE

20CM

73.5CM

BRIM

23 CM

35 CM

CUT SIDE AND BRIM IN BLACK PAPER

SCORE 1CM IN FROM TOP AND BOTTOM AND CUT TABS

GLUE INTO TUBE SHAPE, OVERLAPPING BY 1CM

GLUE BRIM TO TOP OF TUBE

TAPE 23CM PAPER PLATE INSIDE BOTTOM OF TUBE

LINE WITH COLOURED NAPKINS AND FILL WITH CRISPS

Wand Cutlery

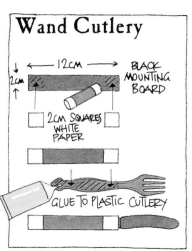

12CM

2CM

BLACK MOUNTING BOARD

2CM SQUARES WHITE PAPER

GLUE TO PLASTIC CUTLERY

YOU **DID** SAY YOUR TABLETOP WAS WASHABLE?

I DON'T THINK ANYTHING'S **THAT** WASHABLE!

Glove Plates

DRAW ROUND HAND ON TO TWO LAYERS OF WHITE PAPER

CUT OUT AND TAPE TO UNDERSIDE OF PAPER PLATE

Dice Napkins

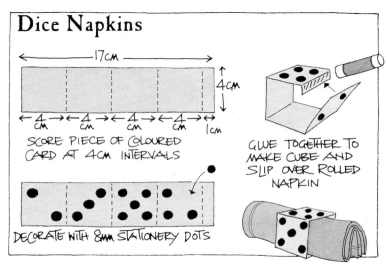

17CM

4CM

4 CM   4 CM   4 CM   4 CM   1CM

SCORE PIECE OF COLOURED CARD AT 4CM INTERVALS

DECORATE WITH 8mm STATIONERY DOTS

GLUE TOGETHER TO MAKE CUBE AND SLIP OVER ROLLED NAPKIN

Starry Cloth

WITH CRAFT KNIFE CUT STAR FROM BASE OF SHOE BOX

SPRAY STARS OVER PAPER TABLECLOTH USING AEROSOL OF METALLIC PAINT

ACTUAL SIZE PATTERN

TRACE ON TO CARD

A Wizard Feast

Magic Beads

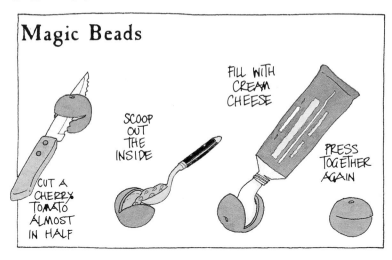

CUT A CHERRY TOMATO ALMOST IN HALF

SCOOP OUT THE INSIDE

FILL WITH CREAM CHEESE

PRESS TOGETHER AGAIN

Cheese Dice

CUT 2CM CUBES FROM VARIOUS FIRM CHEESES

USE BLUNT END OF BAMBOO SKEWER TO MAKE HOLES COPIED FROM REAL DICE

Card Sandwiches

TRIM CRUSTS FROM SANDWICH AND CUT IN HALF

CUT HEARTS, DIAMONDS, CLUBS AND SPADES FROM CARD AND USE TOMATO SAUCE AND YEAST EXTRACT TO STENCIL ON TO SANDWICHES

Cordial Changes

MAKE BLUE ICE CUBES BY PUTTING A DROP OF FOOD COLOURING IN EACH COMPARTMENT BEFORE ADDING WAT

ADD TO RED OR YELLOW FIZZY DRINKS AND WATCH THEM CHANGE COLOUR

Hat Tricks

WITH MELTED CHOCOLATE STICK TOGETHER:

CHOCOLATE OR FONDANT RABBIT

CHOCOLATE BISCUIT

HALVED MINI SWISS ROLL

Chocolate Wands

DIP BOTH ENDS OF CHOCOLATE FINGER BISCUITS INTO MELTED WHITE CHOCOLATE

PLACE ON BAKING PARCHMENT AND LEAVE TO SET

Non-Spill Drink

CE PLASTIC NE GLASSES T AN ANGLE A BOWL LL OF REWED UP APER

FILL TO RIM WITH JELLY AND LEAVE TO SET

WHEN SET, PLACE ON TABLE

Sawn Lady Cakes

TRACE SAW PATTERN ON TO SILVER CARD. COVER SHADED AREA WITH 2CM WIDE COLOURED STICKY TAPE AND CUT OUT

CUT JELLY BABY IN HALF. PRESS INTO FONDANT FANCY AND ADD SAW

SAW ACTUAL SIZE PATTERN

CUT THIS EDGE WITH PINKING SHEARS

On With the Show!

Now comes the high spot of your party – the eagerly awaited magic display, where you get the chance to baffle and bewilder your audience with a selection of the tricks you have learned from this book. Don't try to perform too many illusions in one show, between five and ten is quite enough, and make sure that you have rehearsed them all completely. Write a list of the tricks you have selected, finding a super trick to start off with, and a stupendous one to end your show. You should also make sure that the illusions you have chosen are varied enough so that each one will leave your audience breathless – and remember to never demonstrate any trick twice in the same programme, as someone may begin to get the idea of how it is done.

Look through your list and collect all the props you will need to perform the tricks. If possible, position your table in front of some drawn curtains, and arrange all the chairs for your audience so that they are facing your table, but not too close to it. You may need to prepare some of your illusions away from your audience's gaze, so a screen or an open door nearby would be useful too. As well as providing you with a secret area, you can also use it to make your entrance and exit more dramatic. Keep the lighting dim, and point a gentle light on to your table to direct your audience's attention. Finally, have all your props arranged on (or under) the table, check your costume, call in the audience ... and astonish them!

Index

ALAN DART, the author, began his career designing and making exclusive one-off machine-knitted sweaters for showbusiness personalities, and then started to produce hand-knitting designs and patterns for several women's magazines. He now contributes a wide variety of craft features to many magazines and partwork publications, ranging from toy making to appliqué, papercraft to fabric painting. He has also designed and demonstrated simple craft items for young children on 'Rub a Dub Tub' for TVam, and 'Pob's Programme' for Channel Four. He collaborated with Malcolm Bird on *The Witch's Handbook*, *The Christmas Handbook* and *The Party Handbook*.

MALCOLM BIRD, the illustrator, was discovered by *Honey* magazine, and had his first drawings published whilst he was still at art college studying fashion design. After a thankfully brief career as a designer and pattern cutter, he returned to his first love of drawing, and since then has worked on innumerable magazines, newspapers, and books. His regular commissions have included 'Madge and Beryl', a weekly comic strip for *Jackie* magazine, illustrating Lynda Lee-Potter's column in the *Daily Mail*, and letters page drawings for *Woman's Weekly*.

Photograph by Roger Birch